Philip Osment
BURIED ALIVE

OBERON BOOKS
LONDON

First published in 2001 by Oberon Books Ltd.
(incorporating Absolute Classics)
521 Caledonian Road, London N7 9RH
Tel: 020 7607 3637 / Fax: 020 7607 3629

e-mail: oberon.books@btinternet.com

A catalogue record for this book is available from the British Library.

ISBN: 1 84002 197 7

Cover design: Andrzej Klimowski

Typography: Richard Doust

Printed in Great Britain by Antony Rowe Ltd, Reading.

Characters

MARGARET

ANDREW
her husband

STEWART
their son – eldest child

KATE
their middle child

LIZ
the youngest child

JACK
Margaret's brother

GIOVANNI
a Scot of Italian descent

LUIS
a fifteen year old Brazilian, Stewart's son

AMMY
a journalist in her twenties

ACKNOWLEDGEMENTS

Buried Alive was written for the Method and Madness company of 1998-99 and was developed in consultation with Mike Alfreds and my dramaturg, Noel Greig. This new version of the play was written in 2000-2001 and I would like to thank Mike, Jenny Topper, Jonathan Church and Simon Stokes for their invaluable comments and advice. I would also like to thank Sue Branford for help with the Portuguese; Lin Coghlan; Nina Ward for reading and responding to the play as it came off the printer; and the Peggy Ramsay Foundation for a grant which enabled me to stay solvent and continue working on the script.

Philip Osment
London, 2001

Buried Alive was first performed at the Northcott Theatre, Exeter on 12 March 1999, as a method and Madness production, with the following cast:

MARGARET, Joy Merriman

ANDREW, Jim Pyke

STEWART, David Annen

KATE, Jane Arnfield

LIZ, Louise Bush

JACK, Nigel Whitmey

GIOVANNI, Al Nedjari

LUIS, Antony Ryding

AMMY, Aicha Kossoko

NAT, Eliot Giuralarocca

Director, Mike Alfreds

Designer, Peter McKintosh

Lighting, Natasha Chivers

Sound, Greg Clarke

Assistant Director, Elen Bowman

Dramaturg, Noel Greig

This version of the play opened at the Drum at the Theatre Royal Plymouth on 22 March 2001 and at Hampstead Theatre on 18 April 2001 as a Hampstead Theatre/Plymouth Theatre Royal co-production, with the following cast:

MARGARET, Veronica Roberts

ANDREW, Gary Lilburn

STEWART, Paul Higgins

KATE, Jane Arnfield

LIZ, Louise Bush

JACK, John Ramm

GIOVANNI, Al Nedjari

LUIS, Simon Trinder

AMMY, Michelle Joseph

Director, Mike Alfreds

Designer, Robert Jones

Lighting, Jason Taylor

Sound, Greg Clarke

Assistant director, Robert Hale

The play is set THEN (Edinburgh in the late 1970s) and NOW (Suffolk and Edinburgh in the year 2000)

Scene 1

KATE and LIZ in the bath. They are covered in coal dust and washing each other. THEN. STEWART in bed. NOW.

KATE: (*Singing.*) 'Three wee craws sittin on a waw
    Sittin on a waw Sittin on a waw aw aw aw
    Three wee craws sittin on a waw
    On a cold and frosty morning.'
    (*To LIZ.*) Look at you!
LIZ: Look at *you!*
KATE: 'The first wee craw was greetin for his maw
    Greetin for his maw
    Greetin for his maw aw aw aw
    The first wee craw was greetin for his maw
    On a cold and frosty morning.'
    (*STEWART shoots up in fright.*)
LIZ: Shhh!
KATE: What?
LIZ: I heard something.
KATE: Don't be silly.
LIZ: It's them.
    (*They listen. STEWART looks at his watch.*)
KATE: 'The second wee craw fell and broke his jaw
    Fell and broke his jaw
    Fell and broke his jaw aw aw aw
    The second wee craw fell and broke his jaw
    On a cold and frosty morning.'
    (*STEWART goes to get the whiskey bottle.*)
LIZ: 'The third wee craw couldnae flee at aw
    Couldnae flee at aw
    Couldnae flee at aw aw aw aw
    The third wee craw couldnae flee at aw
    On a cold and frosty morning.'
    (*STEWART drinks the whiskey.*)

Scene 2

*STEWART's cottage in Suffolk. STEWART is morose and getting
drunk. LUIS is playing on his Game Boy and jiggling his leg.*

STEWART: Stop that!

    (*LUIS doesn't respond.*)

    Luis! *Para com isso!*

    (*Still no response.*)

    Eu não vou te falar uma segunda vez!

    (*No response.*)

    Will you fucking stop that!

LUIS: What's wrong?

STEWART: Keep still.

LUIS: This game is shit.

STEWART: You got me to buy it.

LUIS: It's for children. I'm not a child.

    (*STEWART drinks.*)

    There's nothing to do here.

    (*STEWART doesn't respond.*)

    Why can't we go back to London?

STEWART: You know why.

LUIS: Am I a prisoner? You bring me to England and then
you lock me up all day.

STEWART: You're lucky you're not still in Brixton nick on
a shoplifting charge.

    (*LUIS sucks his teeth.*)

    It was only my powers of persuasion that got you off.

LUIS: The police here are like girls. In Brazil the police are
men. In England they are homosexuals.

    (*STEWART laughs.*)

    You wanna take me to Ipswich?

STEWART: What for?

LUIS: You could buy me mobile phone.

STEWART: I'm not getting you a mobile phone.

LUIS: I want with internet.

STEWART: You're not having a mobile.

LUIS: Why not?

STEWART: You don't even know anyone to phone up.
(*LUIS sulks. STEWART drinks.*)
You want to go to Southwold?

LUIS: What for?

STEWART: Swim in the sea.

LUIS: It's too cold for swim in England. I want to go to Ipswich.

STEWART: We're not going to fucking Ipswich.
(*LUIS pulls a face.*)
You were the one who wanted to come and live with me.

LUIS: You don't do anything all day. All you do is drink, drink, drink. You don't answer phone, you switch off mobile. I thought you are photographer. Why you don't take any photos?

STEWART: Because I don't feel like it.

LUIS: Why you don't take me with you to take photos?

STEWART: I'm on holiday.

LUIS: Holiday! In this place!

STEWART: Look, if you don't like it here you can go back to Brazil. You can go back and live with Fernando. Only I seem to remember you kept running away from home. Living on the streets was better than living with Fernando I thought. Mebbe you wanna go back and get knifed by some drug dealer? Is that what you want?

LUIS: You don't care about me. Why you bring me to England if you don't care about me?

STEWART: Of course I care about you.

LUIS: Then take me to Ipswich. Buy me mobile.

STEWART: You're not having a fucking mobile.
(*LUIS throws a chair on the floor.*)
Pick that up!

LUIS: Fuck off

STEWART: Don't you fucking swear at me.
(*AMMY enters.*)

AMMY: Hello?
(*LUIS and STEWART look at her.*)
Sorry, I couldn't get an answer so I came round the back.

STEWART: Right.

AMMY: I'm Ammy.

STEWART: Who?

AMMY: I'm writing the article about your work. Your agent gave me this address.

STEWART: Yeah?

AMMY: I phoned and left a message yesterday.

STEWART: Did you?

AMMY: Didn't you get it?

LUIS: I forgot.

AMMY: If it's not a good time I could –

STEWART: No, it's a great time.

AMMY: Good.

(*They smile at each other. AMMY gets her tape recorder from the bag.*)

It's great to meet you.

STEWART: And you.

AMMY: I've always been a big fan of yours.

STEWART: Really?

AMMY: Yes, when I was still at school we got taken to an exhibition of your photos of Soweto.

STEWART: I see.

AMMY: That was when I decided to do journalism.

STEWART: Well.

(*He smiles at her.*)

You like some wine?

AMMY: I'm driving.

STEWART: Coffee then?

AMMY: Great. White, no sugar.

STEWART: Okay.

LUIS: What about Southwold?

STEWART: What?

LUIS: I thought we go to Southwold.

AMMY: If you've got –

STEWART: It's fine. Why don't you go through to the garden?

(*STEWART goes.*)

AMMY: Marioland?

LUIS: Yes.

AMMY: Great!

LUIS: It's shit.

(*AMMY takes her tape-recorder from her bag and goes to the garden. LUIS looks at the bag. During the scene he goes through it and sees how much money she has.*)

Scene 3

AMMY and STEWART in the garden.

AMMY: Is he…?

STEWART: My son.

AMMY: Oh!

STEWART: Yes.

AMMY: He's not English.

STEWART: His mother was Brazilian.

AMMY: Was?

STEWART: She died last year.

AMMY: I'm sorry.

STEWART: Hadn't seen her for years myself.

AMMY: So now he lives with you?

STEWART: He's come to stay for a while.

AMMY: How old is he?

STEWART: Fifteen.

AMMY: My daughter's four.

(*STEWART nods non-committally.*)

STEWART: So…

AMMY: Yes.

STEWART: This article?

AMMY: Yeah. It's an idea I came up with. There's a lot of interest in your work what with the award and everything and so I went to my editor and suggested I do a piece on you and your work.

STEWART: Right.

AMMY: (*Indicating the tape-recorder.*) You don't mind?

STEWART: No.

AMMY: The photo that won the award?

STEWART: Which one?

AMMY: Of Afghanistan.

STEWART: I meant, "Which award?"

AMMY: The photo of the execution in Afghanistan.

STEWART: Right.

AMMY: They were gay, yeah?

STEWART: They'd been found guilty of buggery so the authorities wanted them to have time to think about their perversion while they died. So they came up with the brilliant idea of burying them in gravel. Good, eh? There'd be all those little pockets of air which would keep them alive longer.

AMMY: Was it a story particularly close to your own heart?

STEWART: I haven't tried buggery myself if that's what you mean. Have you?

AMMY: No.

STEWART: They say it's more pleasurable for men than women. Something to do with stimulation of the prostate gland.

(*She checks her tape recorder.*)

Okay?

AMMY: Yes. It's quite a photo.

STEWART: You think so?

AMMY: Yes. It's the way your eye is drawn to the face as it disappears. It's like you're there with the guy. It's almost as if you're the one burying him.

(*STEWART claps her.*)

STEWART: That's my style. I like to get up close. No tele-photo lens of course. Lots of depth, lots of reality.

AMMY: Didn't you want to do something?

STEWART: Do something?

AMMY: To stop it.

STEWART: There was a Taliban soldier with a gun right behind me. Any backchat and he'd have taken my film off me and killed the guys anyway.

AMMY: What about compassion fatigue?

STEWART: What about it?

AMMY: You know the theory, we're not built to deal with all those images coming at us.

STEWART: No?

AMMY: What do you say to that?

STEWART: Fuck off!

(*She smiles.*)

It's always people who can't be arsed who say things like that.

AMMY: So you're a bit of an idealist?

STEWART: Shhh, don't tell anybody.

(*She laughs.*)

So how about you?

AMMY: What?

STEWART: You're married?

AMMY: No.

STEWART: Single mother.

AMMY: That's right.

STEWART: Boyfriend?

AMMY: Um…sort of.

STEWART: What? Is he married?

(*She laughs.*)

AMMY: So where does it come from?

STEWART: What?

AMMY: You wanting to put the world to rights.

STEWART: I don't know.

AMMY: From your personal experience?

STEWART: I expect so.

AMMY: Your childhood?

STEWART: Probably. You driving back to London tonight?

AMMY: Yes.

STEWART: Pity. Do you know Suffolk?

AMMY: No.

STEWART: There's a great restaurant in the village. Bit late to go to Southwold today but we could go tomorrow.

AMMY: I have to get back.

STEWART: Shame.

AMMY: (*Laughing.*) I wouldn't mind a glass of that wine though.

STEWART: Now you're talking.

(*He goes back to the kitchen where LUIS is sitting. Pours two glasses of wine.*)

LUIS: Are you going to fuck her?

STEWART: Behave yourself.
(*He returns to AMMY.*)

Scene 4

The garden of a nursing home. LIZ is kneeling on a newspaper and talking into a cardboard box. NOW.

LIZ: You getting better, then? No need to be frightened, I'm no going to hurt you. And that naughty pussy cat won't get in here. I promise.
(*She gets a syringe and draws up some water. She gives the bird in the box some water with the syringe.*)
Now, come on, have a wee drink. That's right my darling. You're thirsty, aren't ye? You want some more. That's right. Come on.
(*GIOVANNI enters.*)

GIOVANNI: There you are. Caroline said you were out here.

LIZ: Hello.

GIOVANNI: What have you got there?

LIZ: My bird. A cat caught it and hurt its wing.

GIOVANNI: Let me see. Oh, it's a blackbird.

LIZ: Yes. Caroline says I should have let the cat eat it.

GIOVANNI: Did she?

LIZ: She's no feeling.

GIOVANNI: It doesna seem too badly hurt.

LIZ: (*Opening a tin.*) I found some worms for it. Here you are my darling. Don't you want it? It's a nice fat one. Look.

GIOVANNI: Poor worm!

LIZ: What?

GIOVANNI: There he was this morning happily eating the earth. Then you come along and feed him to the bird!
(*LIZ looks at the worm.*)
It's okay. I'm teasing you.

LIZ: Oh.

GIOVANNI: I've brought you some photos from Donna.

LIZ: Is she back?

GIOVANNI: No, but she sent these and told me to be sure and bring them down for you to see.

LIZ: (*Looking at the photos.*) I got a postcard from her last week. It had a picture of a water buffalo. Who's this boy?

GIOVANNI: Someone she's travelling with.

LIZ: I worry about her. You hear such stories. That girl in Thailand who was murdered.

GIOVANNI: She'll be fine.

LIZ: And then those ones in Australia. Look. That was in yesterday's paper.
(*She holds up the newspaper.*)

GIOVANNI: I don't know why you read those things.
(*Pause.*)
I've got the car. I thought maybe you'd like to go for a drive. We could go down to Jedburgh for our tea.

LIZ: I have to look after the bird.

GIOVANNI: Liz, you're going to have to start going out some day.

LIZ: The cat might come back.

GIOVANNI: Alright, well will we go up to the house and get some tea here?
(*She looks at the box.*)
You want me to ask Caroline if I can bring it down here?

LIZ: I don't like going out.

GIOVANNI: You stay there.
(*He goes.*)

LIZ: Do you not want that worm, my darling. Are you no hungry?

Scene 5

Sound of seagulls. LUIS sits on the beach. STEWART and AMMY run up.

AMMY: My hair's all wet.

STEWART: No point going in the sea without putting your head under.

AMMY: He ducked me Luis.

(*LUIS doesn't respond.*)

STEWART: You should have come in.

LUIS: No way.

AMMY: Bet you were like that as a kid.

STEWART: What?

AMMY: A bully. Just like my brother. He used to do that.

STEWART: You enjoyed it really.

AMMY: Did I?

STEWART: Course you did.

  (*She pushes him over.*)

  Help. Help. Now who's the bully?

  (*They struggle. STEWART can't get the better of her.*)

  Strong aren't you?

AMMY: Am I?

STEWART: Mmmm. I like it.

  (*AMMY and STEWART kiss. LUIS is embarrassed.*)

AMMY: Did you have brothers and sisters?

STEWART: Mmmm? No.

AMMY: Only child?

STEWART: Yeah.

AMMY: Do you ever go back to Scotland?

STEWART: Sometimes. Not much.

AMMY: I'm going up there tomorrow.

STEWART: Oh yeah?

AMMY: Yes, I've been asked to give a talk. They're showing this series of documentaries about Africa and they wanted someone to talk about images of the Third World from a Black perspective. Got to go to Edinburgh for a meeting about it.

STEWART: Very good.

AMMY: So do you still know people up there?

  (*STEWART shakes his head.*)

  No family or anything?

STEWART: No. You fancy a drink?

AMMY: Okay.

STEWART: Lager? Wine?

AMMY: Water. Still.

STEWART: You want anything?

LUIS: Lager.

STEWART: You can't have lager.

(STEWART leaves. AMMY gets out a packet of sweets and offers one to LUIS.)

LUIS: Thanks.

(They both suck their sweets.)

He does not like to talk about Scotland.

AMMY: No?

LUIS: No.

(AMMY looks at him.)

What you wanna know?

AMMY: What?

LUIS: What you wanna know about Stewart?

AMMY: Everything.

LUIS: I could tell you many things.

AMMY: *(Laughing.)* Could you?

LUIS: But I would need some money.

(She laughs.)

AMMY: Luis!

LUIS: Stewart Reid is not his real name. You know that?

AMMY: No.

LUIS: My mother tell me he change his name.

AMMY: I see.

LUIS: What his real name is I don't know. Not even my mother know this. He stayed with her for only a little time.

AMMY: Right.

LUIS: He has an uncle in Edinburgh. He sends him money. I see the letter.

AMMY: An uncle?

LUIS: Yes. *(Getting STEWART's organiser and looking through it.)* Maybe I find you the address.

(She watches him.)

I think maybe Stewart is sick.

AMMY: Sick?

LUIS: He does not work. People phone and he does not answer.

(He is writing the number down.)

There. You want?

AMMY: I…

LUIS: Maybe twenty pounds?

AMMY: No.

> (*STEWART returns swigging from a can. His mood has changed. LUIS hides the organiser. STEWART gives AMMY her water and throws LUIS an ice lolly.*)

AMMY: Thanks.

LUIS: I don't want this.

STEWART: Well don't fucking eat it.

> (*AMMY strokes his leg. He moves it and sits down. She moves up to him and kisses him.*)
>
> So?

STEWART: What?

AMMY: Why do you think you became a photojournalist?

STEWART: Oh for fuck's sake, don't you ever stop working? You know enough now to write your article, don't you? What more do you want to know?

AMMY: Stewart...

STEWART: I'd have thought you'd be able to come up with something quite interesting with all that you found out from last night's in depth research.

AMMY: That's not what last night was about.

STEWART: Your editor should be very impressed. Over and above the call of duty, I'd say. Should get you several rungs up the ladder.

> (*Pause. Suddenly AMMY starts to get dressed. STEWART drinks his lager. LUIS watches them, he still has the piece of paper with the address.*)
>
> Yeah, I'm a bastard. You can put that in your article too.
>
> (*She doesn't respond.*
>
> *He goes towards the sea and sits with his back to them.*
>
> *LUIS holds out the paper to her. She shakes her head.*)

AMMY: Good bye.

LUIS: Good bye.

> *She starts to go.*

STEWART: (*Without looking back.*) Drive carefully.

> (*She stops. Looks at LUIS. Takes a tenner and holds it out to him and he holds out for more. She refuses and he gives her the piece of paper with address. She goes.*)

LUIS is eating his ice lolly and watching STEWART who is looking out to sea.
LIZ and KATE on the beach (North Berwick) as children. THEN.)

LIZ: Stewart!

(*STEWART doesn't respond.*)

KATE: Stewart!

STEWART: What?

LIZ: This seagull can't fly.

(*STEWART goes to them.*)

STEWART: Let me see.

LIZ: Careful.

STEWART: I won't hurt it.

KATE: Poor wee thing.

STEWART: Needs a splint so it does.

(*LUIS throws the stick from his ice lolly away.*)

LIZ: There's a stick from an ice lolly over there.

(*They bend over the bird.*)

Can we keep it? We could take it home with us.

KATE: You know we can't.

STEWART: Gie us your hanky.

(*KATE gives him a handkerchief which he uses to tie the stick on the bird. They are all engrossed.*)

LIZ: We could keep it in the bedroom.

KATE: She won't let you.

LIZ: I could hide it under my coat.

(*Their mother MARGARET, enters with their father, ANDREW. ANDREW has some binoculars. He seems disorientated.*)

MARGARET: What are you doing?

(*The children jump.*)

MARGARET: What have you got there?

LIZ: Nothing.

(*They try to hide the bird.*)

MARGARET: Don't lie, Liz.

(*She approaches them.*)

STEWART: It's a bird that's hurt its wing.

LIZ: I found it.

MARGARET: Ugh! There's no knowing what you could catch off that.

KATE: It's only a bird.

MARGARET: I know what it is. It's filthy. Covered in germs.

LIZ: Look, it's feathers are all soft. Daddy, look.

ANDREW: Eh?

MARGARET: Leave it!

LIZ: Look at the bird I found.

ANDREW: A seagull, is it?

MARGARET: I told you to leave it!

(*LIZ stops stroking the bird.*)

Go and wash your hands.

(*LIZ looks at her and goes.*)

KATE: For God's sake!

MARGARET: What did you say?

KATE: Nothing.

MARGARET: Were you taking the Lord's name in vain?

KATE: No.

MARGARET: You'd better not have been. When I was a girl my father would have knocked me into the middle of next week for doing that. Now away and wash your hands.

(*STEWART and KATE go.*)

ANDREW: It's a seagull.

MARGARET: I can see that.

(*She goes to where the bird is lying in the sand. She looks at it for a moment. She starts covering it with sand. ANDREW watches.*)

Dirty thing.

ANDREW: (*Looking through his binoculars.*) Lots of Soviet submarines in these waters. Have to watch out.

(*The children return.*)

MARGARET: I hope you washed them thoroughly.

LIZ: It was still alive.

MARGARET: What?

LIZ: The seagull. It was still alive.

MARGARET: Away and get your clothes. We'll be late getting your Daddy back to hospital.

ANDREW: It's not time yet.

MARGARET: You have to be back by six or you'll miss your dinner.

(*LIZ is still looking at the place where the bird is buried.*)

MARGARET: Go on, Liz!

LIZ: Why can't Daddy come home with us?

MARGARET: Because he's sick.

(*LIZ goes.*)

(*To KATE.*) You should know better.

KATE: What?

MARGARET: Letting her get germs off that bird.

KATE: I didn't even touch it. Stewart was the one who started messing with it.

(*She starts to go.*)

MARGARET: Are you asking for some time in solitude?

KATE: No.

MARGARET: It's what you need. Some time to reflect on your rudeness and cheek. You can go straight downstairs when we get home. You hear me?

(*KATE goes.*)

STEWART: She didn't do anything.

MARGARET: She's been cheeky all day. She's got to learn. As if I didn't have enough worries.

(*She looks at ANDREW who is looking through his binoculars.*)

Oh, Stewart, what am I going to do?

STEWART: He looks better today.

MARGARET: He lives in a dream world.

(*She starts to cry.*)

It's all that reading he used to do. Used to come home from work and sit reading all night. I could never get an answer out of him. That's what I blame. All those books. Now look at him!

STEWART: He'll be alright.

MARGARET: Mmm. What would I do without you, Stewart?

(*STEWART says nothing.*)

Andrew!

ANDREW: Mmmm?

MARGARET: Come on!

(*They leave.*)

Scene 6

JACK and AMMY. JACK drinks from a can of lager. The television is on in the corner. He chain smokes. NOW.

JACK: Of course I havena seen Stewart hissel now for years.

AMMY: He told me to come and look you up.

JACK: Did he now?

AMMY: Yes. He said, "My Uncle John will remember things I don't remember."

JACK: Uncle Jack.

AMMY: Pardon?

JACK: I was christened John but the family called me Jack.

AMMY: Oh yeah, of course.

JACK: You slipped up there.

AMMY: So was he always interested in photography?

JACK: I wouldn't say that. But he always wanted ta travel. That's why he joined the merchant navy. I helped him there. I had contacts you see. I'd worked on the ships masel. Of course, when I got married to my wife, Eileen, she wasna so keen on me being away all the time. So I got a job on the docks. That's her there.

(*He points to the wall.*)

AMMY: Right.

JACK: She died five years ago.

AMMY: Sorry to hear that.

JACK: Ah well. Where are you from?

AMMY: West Hampstead.

JACK: Sorry?

AMMY: London.

JACK: No I mean, originally.

AMMY: I was born there.

JACK: I see.

AMMY: My parents are from Trinidad.

JACK: Port of Spain. Know it well.

AMMY: So Stewart joined the merchant navy.

JACK: I got him a job as a cook. Assistant cook. Of course the shipping business was already running down by that time. I got made redundant back in the eighties.

AMMY: What did his parents think of him going to sea?

JACK: Oh yes, they thought it was a good idea. Yes, I knew, you know, that he'd gone into the photography business. One of ma pals at work brought in this newspaper – *The Times* or something. It was one of those magazines that they do on Sundays. And there was these photos he'd taken. Ay, they were very good. Terrible, you know. What's the country where they were having the trouble? (*He coughs.*)

AMMY: So you were close to his family.

JACK: I was their uncle.

AMMY: Do they still live here?

JACK: Who?

AMMY: His family.

JACK: No darling. His parents died.

AMMY: Oh right. Any brothers and sisters?

JACK: It was the one where they were having the trouble with the Muslims.

AMMY: You what?

JACK: The photos.

AMMY: He went to Afghanistan a lot.

JACK: Afghanistan.

AMMY: So are you his mother's brother or his father's brother?

JACK: His mother, Margaret, was ma sister.

AMMY: I see. So you and Stewart didn't have the same surname.

JACK: No.

AMMY: I've forgotten what his surname was.

JACK: Afghanistan is where those fanatics took over, isn't it?

AMMY: The Taliban.

JACK: Ay. No, it wasna there. That's where they make all the women cover themselves up.

AMMY: Perhaps it was one of his pieces on Iraq.

JACK: Now, I can't understand that. Making a woman walk around in one of them black sheets with a mask on her face. They don't do that in Trinidad, do they?

AMMY: No.

JACK: It's a crime. Pretty women are there to be admired, do you not think so, Ammy?

AMMY: Some people would say it adds to the mystique.

JACK: Ay, well, you might be right.

(*He laughs and pats her leg. Outburst of coughing.*)

AMMY: I'd like to see his house, where he grew up.

JACK: Would you?

AMMY: I'm trying to understand what motivates him to do the work he does.

JACK: I see. I see. Was it Iran? Did he go to Iran?

AMMY: He might have done.

JACK: It might have been Iran.

AMMY: So any information that you could give me would be very useful. You know, to round out the picture.

JACK: I see.

(*He coughs again.*)

How much will you be paying, Ammy?

AMMY: Well, as I explained, I'm not writing like an investigative piece. It's more for the Arts Page.

JACK: So are you no getting paid?

AMMY: Well, yeah.

JACK: I'd like to help you, Ammy, you're a lovely lassie but it wouldna be right to just talk to you without it being a business arrangement. You know what I mean? It's eh…what do they call it? No copyright…you have to pay for stories nowadays, don't you?

AMMY: Is there a story?

JACK: It's just a way of talking.

(*AMMY takes out her wallet.*)

AMMY: So how much then?

JACK: Well, I don't know…

AMMY: Twenty pounds?

JACK: Twenty pounds?

AMMY: Thirty?

JACK: You know darling, I think mebbe we should leave it.

AMMY: If you want more I'd have to talk to my editor.

JACK: I canna take your money, darling.

AMMY: You can't?

JACK: I'm sorry. It wouldna be right.
  (*He coughs.*)
  Excuse me, darling.
  (*He spits into his handkerchief.*)
  (*Pointing to the cigarette.*) That's these things. I should give them up, but, you know…

AMMY: Yeah.

JACK: It's been nice meeting you, Ammy. Always pleased to meet a pretty girl.

AMMY: (*Giving him her card.*) Well, look, if you change your mind…

JACK: Ay right.
  (*He gets up to see her out. He coughs again.*)

AMMY: It's okay.

JACK: Right you are. Goodbye, darling.

AMMY: Goodbye.
  (*She goes. He stops coughing. He gets up and puts on his coat to go out.*)

Scene 7

MARGARET is playing patience. ANDREW is trying to read. LIZ is doing homework. THEN.

ANDREW: There! Hear it?

LIZ: No.

MARGARET: What time is it?
  (*LIZ goes and looks at the clock.*)

LIZ: Half past seven.

MARGARET: Where's he got to?

ANDREW: Can you no hear them?
  (*LIZ listens.*)

LIZ: I can't hear anything, Daddy? Mum?

MARGARET: What now?

LIZ: Is it time to let Kate out yet?
  (*MARGARET goes on playing her cards.*)
  Can I let her out, Mum?

(*No response.*)

You said if I did my jobs you'd let me.

MARGARET: It won't do her any harm to stay down there a bit longer.

LIZ: But –

MARGARET: Do you want to go down there?

LIZ: No.

ANDREW: (*To the wall.*) I can't read my book. Ye hear me? (*ANDREW bangs on the wall.*)

MARGARET: Stop it!

LIZ: There's nothing there, Daddy.

(*LIZ continues with her homework.*)

MARGARET: (*Holding up the key.*) Here!

(*LIZ runs to get it and exits.*)

Hope nothing's happened to him.

ANDREW: Who?

MARGARET: Who? Stewart! Who do you think?

ANDREW: Where is he?

MARGARET: Out with that boy from the Italian restaurant.

ANDREW: Ah.

(*He bangs on the wall.*)

MARGARET: Andrew!

ANDREW: Mmmm?

MARGARET: That's enough!

ANDREW: I can't concentrate on my book.

(*LIZ returns with the key.*)

MARGARET: Where is she?

LIZ: She's coming.

ANDREW: They kept me awake half the night last night. They were running up and down the stairs, knocking on my wall. Then they were talking and whispering. All night long.

LIZ: Was it Mrs Goldstein, Daddy?

ANDREW: Ay.

(*KATE enters.*)

MARGARET: Go on.

(*KATE kneels.*)

KATE: Jesus, I ask forgiveness for my sins.

MARGARET: And?

KATE: And I will try harder to be good.

MARGARET: You better had. Get up!

(*KATE gets up.*)

KATE: Is there anything t'eat?

MARGARET: You think we're made of money?

LIZ: There's some cake Mrs Goldstein gave me.

MARGARET: What?

LIZ: It's got cherries in it.

MARGARET: You took it?

LIZ: Yes.

MARGARET: How often have I told you not to take anything from that woman? You want folk to say I'm a bad mother and I don't give you enough to eat? Is that what you want? Is it?

LIZ: No.

MARGARET: You want to be put in a children's home?

LIZ: No.

MARGARET: Because that's what they'll do to you my girl, if you go around telling folk you don't get enough to eat.

LIZ: I don't tell people that.

KATE: It's just a wee bit of fruit cake.

(*MARGARET looks at her menacingly.*

Knock at the door.)

MARGARET: Go and see who that is.

(*KATE goes.*)

(*Calling after her.*) Make sure they don't see you. (*To LIZ.*) It will be the people from the council come to take you away for what you've been saying about me.

LIZ: I haven't been saying anything.

(*KATE returns.*)

KATE: It's Uncle Jack. Shall I let him in?

MARGARET: Go on.

(*KATE goes again.*)

Drew.

ANDREW: Mmm?

MARGARET: Give me the stick.

ANDREW: What?

MARGARET: The stick.

(*He gives it to her. She puts it away.*
KATE returns with JACK.)

JACK: There ye are then.

MARGARET: You been to the races?

JACK: Just back. How are you, Andy?

ANDREW: Fine, Jack. Fine.

JACK: You're looking better.

ANDREW: I canna read. It's all the talking.

JACK: The talking?

MARGARET: They're paper thin, these walls.

JACK: And there's Lizzie.

LIZ: Hello, Uncle Jack.

JACK: And how are you, Katy?

KATE: Okay.

JACK: I'm sure those legs of yours are an inch longer every
time I see you.

(*KATE laughs.*)

MARGARET: Pull your skirt down.

(*KATE pulls her skirt down.*)

You'll have had your tea.

JACK: I've not been home yet.

MARGARET: We've just had ours.

JACK: (*Looking for signs of tea.*) Oh yes?

MARGARET: Steak and kidney pie. But this greedy lot ate
the whole thing up.

ANDREW: (*In response to something he has heard in the wall.*)
Huh!

JACK: Eileen will have something for me.

MARGARET: I'd offer you some tea but they drank all the
milk.

JACK: Was that you, Lizzie?

LIZ: What?

JACK: That drank all the milk.

LIZ: No.

ANDREW: They've got it switched on again.

MARGARET: Drew!

JACK: What's that, Andy?

28

ANDREW: Oh hello, Jack. How you doing?

JACK: Fine.

ANDREW: Been to the races, have you?

JACK: Ay. Won forty and lost fifty.

ANDREW: (*Laughing.*) Hah!

JACK: But I took thirty wi me so I'm in pocket.

MARGARET: How do you make that out?

JACK: (*Winking at KATE.*) I've still got two ten pound notes in my wallet.

MARGARET: If Daddy knew you'd end up throwing your money away gambling!

ANDREW: They've got a transmitter next door, you know.

JACK: A transmitter?

(*He winks at KATE again. She giggles.*)

ANDREW: They can make their voices come out of my radio. Even when it's switched off.

JACK: (*Smiling at KATE.*) Why are they doing that, Andy?

ANDREW: I think they're trying to recruit me.

(*KATE and JACK can hardly control their giggles. LIZ kicks KATE.*)

KATE: Aowh!

LIZ: Stop laughing.

KATE: You wee beastie.

MARGARET: Here!

(*They stop.*
STEWART enters. He looks anxiously at MARGARET.)

JACK: Ah, here he is! Hello, Stewart.

STEWART: Hi.

LIZ: You're late.

STEWART: Giovanni's Mum made me stay to dinner.

JACK: You missed steak and kidney pie.

STEWART: What?

(*Awkward pause.*)

JACK: Well, I just came to see if you were okay.

MARGARET: We're fine.

JACK: Better get back before Eileen sends out a search party. She'll be thinking I've got a fancy woman.

(*Nobody responds.*)

Bye then, Andy.

ANDREW: You off, Jack?

JACK: Ay.

ANDREW: Don't let them see you.

JACK: Who?

ANDREW: Next door. They'll be onto you. (*Confidentially.*) KGB.

JACK: Right. Don't I get a kiss, Lizzie?

(*LIZ kisses him.*)

(*Surreptitiously.*) Here.

(*He gives her some chocolate. LIZ hides it.*)

Stewart.

(*JACK goes, pulling a face at STEWART about MARGARET. KATE sees him out.*)

MARGARET: Give it here.

LIZ: What?

MARGARET: You know what.

LIZ: I don't.

MARGARET: You want some time downstairs? You know you're not allowed chocolate.

(*LIZ gives MARGARET the bar of chocolate.*)

STEWART: (*To MARGARET.*) Giovanni's mother made me stay. I couldn't get out of it.

LIZ: What did she give you t'eat?

STEWART: Pasta. (*Looking at MARGARET.*) It wasn't very nice.

(*KATE returns looking flushed.*)

MARGARET: What have you been doing?

KATE: Nothing.

STEWART: (*To MARGARET.*) I'm sorry I was late.

(*ANDREW has got the stick back and bangs on the wall.*)

MARGARET: (*Cracking.*) Stop it! Stop it!

STEWART: Dad!

(*He takes the stick from him.*)

ANDREW: They're trying to brainwash me, son.

MARGARET: I'm away to my bed.

(*She goes. The three children look at each other.*)

STEWART: Mum! Mum!

(*He goes.*)

Scene 8

GIOVANNI is sitting at a restaurant table doing his accounts. JACK stands before him. NOW.

JACK: Nice place, Giovanni. I heard you were doing well.

GIOVANNI: I'm okay. Gets busy this time of year with the tourists and the Festival.

JACK: You run it on your own?

GIOVANNI: I've got staff. A manager.

JACK: Right.

GIOVANNI: And Donna helps out.

JACK: She's okay, is she?

GIOVANNI: Donna? Ay.

JACK: I just wondered how she was.

GIOVANNI: She's twenty.

JACK: Yes. She must be. Any other children?

GIOVANNI: No.

JACK: Ah.

GIOVANNI: Something else we've got in common. My wife, Maria, couldna have kids.

JACK: Eh? Oh yes. So she works here, Donna?

GIOVANNI: Not at the moment. She's away round the world, travelling. Last time I heard from her she was in India.

JACK: India! Never liked the place.

GIOVANNI: You know it?

JACK: I know Bombay.

GIOVANNI: She loves it.

JACK: I just wondered, you know, how she was.

GIOVANNI: After all these years?

JACK: Well…

GIOVANNI: She's fine. She's a good girl.

JACK: Did you ever tell her…?

GIOVANNI: What?

JACK: About her mother.

GIOVANNI: Ay, I told her.

JACK: I don't suppose she sees Liz at all.

GIOVANNI: They write.

JACK: That's good. Only uh...well, there was this journalist came and spoke to me. She wants to write about Stewart's life. Never trusted journalists, not after...

GIOVANNI: No.

JACK: I just wondered if she'd been to see you.

GIOVANNI: No.

JACK: Well, I just thought you should know.

GIOVANNI: Scared what I was going to say to her, were you?

JACK: You what?

GIOVANNI: I wouldnae dae anything t'hurt Donna, Jack.

JACK: Right.

GIOVANNI: So you've no need to worry.

JACK: Well, you'll know if she comes looking for you.

GIOVANNI: Ay.

JACK: She's a darkie. You won't be able to miss her.

GIOVANNI: Right.

JACK: Unless she comes by night! Eh?

GIOVANNI: Yes.

(*Pause.*)

JACK: Well...

GIOVANNI: See you in another twenty years, Jack.

JACK: Ay, mebbe.

(*He goes. GIOVANNI watches him.*)

Scene 9

LIZ and KATE's bedroom. STEWART appears. THEN.

KATE: What are you doing creeping around the house?

(*He opens his hand and shows them the chocolate.*)

You didn't!

STEWART: I did.

KATE: From the dustbin?

STEWART: Yes.

(*The two girls stare at him.*)

Well, come on then.

LIZ: Will it no be dirty?

STEWART: No, Lizzie, it's no dirty. Oh Lord, we thank Thee for this gift from Thy servant Jack. In your wisdom, Lord, you have seen fit that it should be rescued from the dark void of our dustbin and should find its way into the stomachs of these Thy handmaidens.
(*LIZ giggles.*)

STEWART: Put your tongues out.

LIZ: Why?

STEWART: It's what the Catholics do when they say mass.

LIZ: We're not Catholics.

STEWART: And this isn't the body of Christ. Now put your tongues out.
(*LIZ puts her tongue out. STEWART puts a piece of chocolate on it.*
KATE puts her tongue out. He does the same for her.)
Savour it. Feel it melting on your tongue and releasing all its flavour onto your taste buds.
(*He puts some on his own tongue.*)
Mmmm.

LIZ: Mmmm.

KATE: It just makes things worse.

STEWART: What?

KATE: Having a wee bit of chocolate.

STEWART: Thus spake the pessimist.

LIZ: I like Uncle Jack.

STEWART: Yes.

LIZ: Do you like him, Kate?

KATE: He's okay.

STEWART: What was he saying to you when he went out tonight?

KATE: Nothing.

STEWART: I heard him say something on the doorstep.

KATE: Just that he's going to take me racing at Musselburgh one day.

LIZ: Really? I want to go.

KATE: You can't you're too young.

STEWART: You know what Mum thinks of gambling.

KATE: So?

STEWART: You'll be in trouble.

KATE: So will you if Uncle Jack gets you that job.

STEWART: Shut it.

LIZ: A job? What doing?

STEWART: Just a job. Get back to your bed and we'll go out for our dinner.

LIZ: What sort of job?

STEWART: Get back to your bed.

KATE: Uncle Jack said he'll get him a job on a ship.

LIZ: On a ship? You mean go to sea?

STEWART: I went out for my dinner and I had...

LIZ: Are you going to sea, Stewart?

STEWART: Of course not.

LIZ: I don't want you to go away.

STEWART: (*To KATE.*) Now look what you've done. I went out for my dinner and I had a big steak. (*To LIZ.*) Come on, your go.

(*She doesn't respond.*)

KATE: I went out for my dinner and I had a big steak and a fresh pineapple.

STEWART: Come on.

LIZ: No.

STEWART: I'm no going away.

LIZ: You are.

STEWART: I'm not. It was just one of Uncle Jack's mad ideas. Now tell us what you'll have. Some fish fingers?

LIZ: No.

STEWART: Some baked beans?

LIZ: No.

STEWART: What then?

LIZ: A bag of chips.

STEWART: Liz went out for her dinner and she had a big steak, a fresh pineapple and a bag of chips. I went out for my dinner and I had a big steak, a fresh pineapple, a bag of chips and lasagne.

LIZ: What's that?

KATE: I went out for my dinner and I had a big steak, a fresh pineapple, a bag of chips, lasagne and some roast chicken.

LIZ: I went out for my dinner and I had a big steak, a fresh
pineapple, a bag of chips, lassie Anna –
(*STEWART and KATE try to contain their laughter.*)
…some roast chicken and a strawberry ice cream.
(*STEWART and KATE laugh.*)
Stop laughing at me.
MARGARET: (*Off.*) What's going on in there?
KATE: Nothing.
MARGARET: Go to sleep.
KATE: Okay.
(*STEWART signals that he must go. KATE nods and signals
him to be quiet.*)
LIZ: You won't go away, will you, Stewart?
KATE: Shhh!
STEWART: No, Liz.
LIZ: You promise?
STEWART: Yes, I promise.

Scene 10

AMMY is talking on her mobile. NOW.

AMMY: You got my fax?
What did you think of the article?
I do like his photos. Doesn't mean I have to like him.
Nothing went on between us! You've just got a suspicious
mind. What I wanted to say was, can you hold on to it
for a bit?
I want to find out a bit more about him. There's a bigger
story there I just know. I've been doing a bit of detective
work.
(*She laughs.*)
Well, I was sure the uncle was hiding something, he
couldn't wait to get rid of me and then I saw him
hurrying down the street just after I'd left him coughing
his lungs up in his chair. So I followed him.
(*She laughs.*)
To this Italian restaurant.
It was closed. There was only the manager there.

They just talked for a while and it looked quite... I don't know... sort of intense. Then he left.

From a telephone box across the road!

Who's Miss Marple?

Oh right. Anyway I'm sure there's more to find out so if you could wait a bit –

Well, if I don't, you've got what I've written already and you can use that.

I miss you as well.

I can't see you Friday. I have to go to my Mum's pick up Bonny.

Next week I'm coming back up to Edinburgh, I'm giving that talk, remember? Anyway I thought you were going to Paris with your wife. What about Sunday?

Oh. Well, maybe, my Mum will keep Bonny and I could pick her up on Saturday.

Yeah. Yeah, and you. Oh, and Alan? See if anybody knows Stewart's real surname.

Scene 11

GIOVANNI and STEWART. STEWART is looking through binoculars. THEN.

GIOVANNI: Stewart McNulty.

STEWART: What?

GIOVANNI: You're a pervert.

STEWART: I'm not. I just like watching people. Look at those two. He's just got in from work and he went to kiss her and she turned her head away.

GIOVANNI: I want to see the ships.

(*STEWART hands him the binoculars.*)

STEWART: I love it. It's like you're watching a film. You can see right into their lives.

GIOVANNI: Greek tanker.

STEWART: Where?

GIOVANNI: (*Handing the binoculars back.*) Just coming in.

STEWART: It's Soviet.

GIOVANNI: How do you know?

STEWART: Those are Russian letters on the side.

GIOVANNI: So what do you think?

STEWART: What about?

GIOVANNI: Your uncle getting us both a job on the Rio de Janeiro.

STEWART: Mebbe.

GIOVANNI: Ask him.

STEWART: Funny, isn't it? All these ships coming in and out of Leith from all over the world and the same time there's people in they houses who've never been out of Edinburgh. Like those two sitting there having their tea. Oh, she's crying.

GIOVANNI: Who is?

STEWART: The woman.

GIOVANNI: My Dad never wants to go anywhere. It was such an effort for him to come here in the first place he never wants to travel again.

STEWART: He goes back to Italy.

GIOVANNI: That doesna count. I've got cousins in Manhattan, you know that.

STEWART: You told me.

GIOVANNI: If we joined the merchant navy I could take you to visit. Imagine.

STEWART: What about your family?

GIOVANNI: What about them?

STEWART: Your Dad wants you to take over the restaurant. He told me.

GIOVANNI: No way. That one's Greek.
   (*He hands the binoculars back to STEWART.*)

STEWART: And what about that Maria in Naples?

GIOVANNI: Who told you about her?

STEWART: Your Mum. Thought you were supposed to marry her and have lots of bambini.

GIOVANNI: What are you going to do? Stay in Edinburgh and work in a bank?

STEWART: (*Sings.*) 'You're the one girl in town I'd marry.'

GIOVANNI: Stop that.
   (*He attacks STEWART.*)

STEWART: Alright. Look, they're kissing now. He's got his hand inside her blouse.

GIOVANNI: You are a pervert.

(*GIOVANNI takes the binoculars.*
KATE enters.)

KATE: There you are!

(*They both jump guiltily.*)

STEWART: What do you want?

KATE: Mum wants you.

(*GIOVANNI is looking at the ships again.*)
(*Mouthed at STEWART so that GIOVANNI can't here.*)
You're in trouble.

STEWART: (*Also mouthed.*) Why?

KATE: (*Pointing at her watch and mouthing.*) Because you're late.

(*They look at GIOVANNI.*)
Are those Dad's binoculars?

STEWART: Ay.

GIOVANNI: Sorry.

KATE: It's okay.

GIOVANNI: Take them.

KATE: You were using them.

GIOVANNI: I've finished. Here.

KATE: No.

STEWART: Oh, for God's sake!

(*He takes the binoculars and puts them in their case.*)
I've got to go.

GIOVANNI: Are you no coming to eat at my place? My Mum's expecting you.

STEWART: I can't.

GIOVANNI: I'll walk with you then. I've never been to your house.

STEWART: It's out of your way.

GIOVANNI: It doesna matter.

STEWART: We have to get some messages on the way home.

GIOVANNI: Okay.

STEWART: See you tomorrow.

GIOVANNI: You still coming to the pictures?

STEWART: I'll try.

GIOVANNI: It's okay, I'll treat you.

KATE: What film?

STEWART: *Star Wars.*

GIOVANNI: You want to come?

STEWART: (*Together.*) She wouldn't like it.

KATE: (*Together.*) I don't know if –

GIOVANNI: You seen it?

KATE: No.

GIOVANNI: Well, come on then. I'll treat you as well.
  (*KATE looks at STEWART.*)

KATE: I could say I have to stay on at school for something.

STEWART: We're going to the evening show.

GIOVANNI: We can go to the early one.
  (*KATE looks at STEWART. He shrugs.*)

STEWART: It's up to you, if you think…

KATE: Yeah, alright then.

STEWART: Come on.

GIOVANNI: Right. Four o'clock tomorrow outside the Odeon.

KATE: Okay.

STEWART: See ya.

GIOVANNI: Bye Kate.

KATE: Bye.

Scene 12

The nursing home. Night. NOW.
LIZ enters in her dressing gown and goes to the bird.

LIZ: You okay, my darling? I heard the cats outside my window and I thought you'd be frightened. I won't let them harm you. Go back to sleep now. Shhh there's Caroline. I must have woken her up. Everyone in here thinks I'm mad coming out here talking to you. They don't understand, do they? They say you're just a bird. Well, they're just people. You can't trust people. They're dangerous. They lie in wait for you with sharp claws and great big white teeth. And if you're not careful they'll catch you and tear you apart. So you have to watch out and not let them get too close.

Scene 13

ANDREW in just a long shirt outside MARGARET's bedroom door. THEN.

ANDREW: Margaret! Margaret!

(*Pause.*)

Margaret! Let me in!

(*STEWART enters.*)

STEWART: Dad!

ANDREW: Margaret!

STEWART: You're waking everybody up.

ANDREW: Go back to your bed. Margaret!

(*KATE and LIZ get up to see what is happening.*)

KATE: Dad!

ANDREW: Leave me alone!

KATE: She's taken one of her sleeping pills, Dad.

ANDREW: I want to go in with her.

LIZ: Why can't you sleep in your own room, Daddy?

(*The following exchange between KATE and LIZ runs simultaneously with ANDREW and STEWART's dialogue.*)

KATE: Go back to your bed, Lizzie.

LIZ: You go back to your bed.

KATE: Come on, Liz.

LIZ: No!

KATE: Liz!

(*The following dialogue between ANDREW and STEWART runs simultaneously with the previous exchange between LIZ and KATE.*)

ANDREW: Margaret!

STEWART: Dad! Come on!

ANDREW: She's my wife. It's my right, you know!

STEWART: She's asleep, Dad.

ANDREW: She can wake up.

(*KATE is pulling LIZ one way. STEWART is pulling his father the other.*)

KATE: (*Simultaneously with ANDREW.*) Liz, will you come on?

ANDREW: (*Simultaneously with KATE.*) Get off me.

LIZ: Leave me alone, you bully.

(*ANDREW hits out at STEWART. STEWART falls to the floor. LIZ and KATE look on, shocked.*
MARGARET gets up. She is very bleary eyed.)

MARGARET: What's going on?

KATE: Nothing.

ANDREW: I'm coming in your room tonight.

MARGARET: You are not!

ANDREW: Yes I am!

KATE: Dad!

MARGARET: You can keep out of my room.

(*He tries to grab her.*)

Get off me! You're disgusting.

ANDREW: Come on.

(*MARGARET hits him.*)

MARGARET: Get him back to his room.

STEWART: Dad.

KATE: Go on, Dad.

MARGARET: You two can get back into bed as well.

KATE: Alright?

STEWART: Ay.

MARGARET: Go on.

(*LIZ and Kate go.*)

ANDREW: It's never right.

(*MARGARET turns and goes back into her room.*)

What sort of life is it if you can't get in your own wife's bed?

STEWART: (*Guiding him back to his room.*) Dad, for God's sake! It's three o'clock in the morning.

ANDREW: (*Shouting at MARGARET's door.*) What am I supposed to do? Eh?

STEWART: Shhh.

ANDREW: What would you do?

(*He goes. STEWART returns to his room. On his way,*

MARGARET stops him.)

MARGARET: Is he back in bed?

STEWART: Yes.

MARGARET: I can't live like this. My father warned me.

STEWART: I'm away to my bed.

MARGARET: I won't be getting any sleep now.

STEWART: *(Reluctantly.)* You want me to sit up with you?

MARGARET: You're a good boy.

(MARGARET sits as STEWART makes her tea.
KATE and LIZ – their bedroom. THEN.)

LIZ: What's he like?

KATE: Very dark. His parents are Italian.

LIZ: Does that mean he's Catholic?

KATE: Ay.

LIZ: Kate!

KATE: He's got this line of hair that starts here *(Pointing to just below the neck.)* and it spreads out here *(She indicates between her breasts.)* and then thins out again and it goes in a line down to his belly button and then down again until…

LIZ: Until what?

KATE: Well, it goes right down.

LIZ: To his thingy?

KATE: Ay, to "his thingy"! And when I touch him here on his side he gets these goose bumps. You can see them come up on him. It's amazing. If I touch him, he gets goose bumps.

LIZ: Do you get goose bumps if he touches you?

KATE: Mmmm.

(LIZ strokes herself dreamily.)

And it makes you forget everything bad that's ever happened to you. Just being there with him. It gives you this feeling in your stomach that's like a pang for the future.

LIZ: What's a pang?

KATE: It's like a pain.

LIZ: It's a bad feeling?

KATE: No. You know that the future's there and there's all these things you're going to feel and experience and they've rolled themselves up into a tight wee ball that's there in your stomach waiting to burst open. It's like you know there's this whole world out there waiting for you.

LIZ: Would you go away and leave me?

KATE: What?

LIZ: Would you?

KATE: Of course not.

LIZ: Is Stewart going away?

KATE: No! Now get to sleep.

(*Downstairs. MARGARET is drinking her tea. STEWART can barely keep awake.*)

MARGARET: If I thought you'd ever do anything like that, Stewart.

STEWART: What?

MARGARET: Treat a woman like some "thing" to gratify yourself with. And he never washes. You know, down there.

(*Pause.*)

You ought to go down and see that bank manager. See what trainees they're taking on.

STEWART: Mr Dean thinks I should have applied to University.

MARGARET: You can take exams down at the bank.

STEWART: He says there's this course in Manchester.

MARGARET: Come here.

STEWART: What?

(*He goes to her. She goes to squeeze a blackhead on his face.*)

It's okay.

MARGARET: I'll get it out.

(*She squeezes the blackhead out.*)

There.

(*She shows it to him. She strokes his hair. STEWART is unable to get away.*)

You'd like it at the bank. You don't want to go all the way to Manchester, do you?

STEWART: I don't know.

MARGARET: What good did University do your father? Look at him.

Scene 14

Fairground music. KATE and GIOVANNI on the big wheel. THEN.

KATE: Giovanni.

GIOVANNI: What?

KATE: I like saying it.

GIOVANNI: Oh.

KATE: Giovanni.

GIOVANNI: Kate.

KATE: Giovanni.

GIOVANNI: Kate.

KATE: Giovanni, Giovanni, Giovanni.

GIOVANNI: Kate, Kate, Kate.

> (*He rocks their seat. She screams.*)

KATE: Don't.

> (*He rocks it more.*)
> You'll have us out of this!
> (*He holds her.*)
> Giovanni.
> (*She kisses him.*)

GIOVANNI: Kate.

> (*He kisses her.*)

KATE: I have to get back.

GIOVANNI: It's not that late.

KATE: I'm not supposed to be out.

GIOVANNI: Why not?

KATE: I'm supposed to go straight home after school.

GIOVANNI: I'll take you.

KATE: No!

GIOVANNI: Why not?

KATE: I don't want you ever to come to my house.

GIOVANNI: You ashamed of me?

KATE: No. But you must never come there. Promise me you never will!

GIOVANNI: Okay.

> (*Pause.*)
> Perhaps it's broken down. We'll have to stay up her all night.

KATE: You think?
GIOVANNI: Mebbe.
(*He puts her hand on his lap.*)
That feels good.
(*She puts his hand on her breast.*)
KATE: I wish I could.
GIOVANNI: What?
KATE: Stay up here forever.

Scene 15

LUIS and STEWART. STEWART has a towel around him and is holding some money. NOW.

STEWART: Where did you get it?
(*LUIS doesn't say anything.*)
Come on! It's not from my wallet so where did it come from?
LUIS: I don't know.
STEWART: If you're going to stay in England and live with me you're going to have to change your ways. Like you can start telling the truth.
LUIS: I tell the truth.
STEWART: You stole this, didn't you?
LUIS: No.
STEWART: Where'd you get it?
LUIS: The woman.
STEWART: What woman?
LUIS: The writer woman. The one you fuck.
STEWART: You thieved off her?
LUIS: She give it me.
STEWART: Pull the other one. Why would she give you money?
LUIS: I don't know. Maybe she feel sorry for me because my father is drunk all the time.
STEWART: You don't have to stay with me.
LUIS: Huh! My mother told me you don't care about nobody. You don't care about her, you don't care about me.

STEWART: Get to your room.

LUIS: What?

STEWART: Bedroom. Now!

> (*LUIS sucks his teeth.*)

> Get to your fucking room!

> (*LUIS goes.*

> *STEWART gets in the bath.*

> *MARGARET enters with a towel. STEWART is embarrassed.*

> *THEN.*)

MARGARET: What's this?

STEWART: (*Covering himself up.*) A towel.

MARGARET: What was it doing under your bed?

> (*STEWART doesn't answer. LIZ and KATE are watching*
> *from the landing.*)

> It was down between the bed and the wall. What was it
> doing there?

STEWART: I don't know.

MARGARET: Look at the state of it! That's one of my best
towels. It's all stuck together. What were you doing with
it down the side of your bed?

> (*STEWART doesn't respond.*)

> Eh?

> (*No response.*)

> Ay, you might well not answer me. Are you a pig? Is
that what you are?

STEWART: No.

MARGARET: Get downstairs.

STEWART: What?

MARGARET: Downstairs now!

> (*ANDREW comes to see what's going on.*)

> What are you waiting for? Go on!

STEWART: No.

MARGARET: You what?

STEWART: I'm not going down there.

MARGARET: Oh, are you no? You think you're too
grand now, do you? You think you're too clever? Mebbe
I should take this up to your school and show your
teacher. See how grand and clever they think you are
then. Do you want me to do that?

STEWART: No.

MARGARET: Then get down in that cellar!

STEWART: No.

MARGARET: (*To ANDREW.*) You hear that? You hear him? Treating me like dirt! Treating his own mother like dirt! To think I thought you weren't going to be like the rest of them! After all the sacrifices I've made for you!

STEWART: I didn't ask you to make any sacrifices.

MARGARET: (*To ANDREW.*) Listen to him! Did you hear him?

ANDREW: Margaret.

MARGARET: Don't Margaret me! You stand there looking on. Not raising a finger to help me bring up these children. And then they treat me like dirt.

ANDREW: Calm down.

MARGARET: Calm down! He tells me to calm down! It will be the death of me, this family. (*To STEWART.*) "Honour thy father and thy mother," do they not teach you that at that wonderful school of yours? Eh? This is the gratitude! This is the thanks!

ANDREW: (*Reaching out to her.*) Margaret.

MARGARET: (*Screaming.*) Don't touch me!
(*He reaches out again.*)
(*Screaming.*) Get off me! Get off me!
(*She continues to scream.*)

ANDREW: Get downstairs, laddie!

STEWART: No.
(*MARGARET screams again.*)

ANDREW: Go on.

STEWART: No! I'm not going to let her terrorise me any more.

MARGARET: Terrorise you! What do you mean terrorise you?

STEWART: That's what you do. (*Pointing at LIZ and KATE.*) You do it to them! (*Pointing at ANDREW.*) You do it to him! Why do you think he never gets better? It's probably because of you that he went mad in the first fucking place. (*They all look at STEWART in shock.*)

I'm sorry. I didna mean it. Mum.
(*He goes to touch her.*)

MARGARET: Get out of this house.

ANDREW: Margaret.

MARGARET: Go on! We don't need you here. You can go!

STEWART: (*Coldly.*) Ah well, I just might.

ANDREW: Stewart, laddie.

STEWART: Uncle Jack can get me a job.

MARGARET: Huh!

STEWART: On the Rio de Janeiro.

MARGARET: Following in his footsteps, are you? (*Thrusting the towel at KATE.*) Here, take this and wash it.
(*KATE goes.*)
I'll be glad to be rid of you.
(*She goes.*)

STEWART: (*Furiously.*) I hate her! I hate her! I hate her!

ANDREW: (*Patting him.*) Your mother doesna mean it, son. You think it over.

STEWART: What? And end up like you?
(*ANDREW withdraws as if stung.*)
Mother! I'm leaving and I'm never coming back! You hear me?

LIZ: (*Throwing herself on STEWART and hitting him.*) You promised you wouldn't go! I hope I never see you again.
(*She rushes out.*
STEWART puts his head in his hands.
LUIS enters. NOW.)

LUIS: Stewart?

STEWART: What?

LUIS: I didn't steal. She give it me.
(*Pause.*)

STEWART: How would you like to go to Scotland?

LUIS: Scotland?

STEWART: Yes.

LUIS: Why?

STEWART: See where I grew up.

LUIS: No.

STEWART: Why not?

LUIS: I want to go back to London.

STEWART: Well you can't.

   (*LUIS sulks.*)

   We could go over to Felixstowe, see if there's any ships going up to Leith. Make an adventure of it.

LUIS: What sort of ship?

STEWART: A merchant ship. Like the ones I used to work on. I could pull a few strings, get us a cabin. Might even be able to track down my sister while we're up there.

LUIS: I didn't know you had a sister.

STEWART: Yes.

LUIS: What's her name?

STEWART: Liz.

   (*LUIS says nothing.*)

   Well, come on!

LUIS: What?

STEWART: Meet me halfway for fuck's sake!

LUIS: I don't want to go to Scotland.

STEWART: Well too bad! We're going.

LUIS: Why you ask me when you already decide?

   (*He goes.*

   STEWART gets dressed and packs an old kit bag.)

Scene 16

GIOVANNI's restaurant. NOW.
AMMY has eaten and is finishing her wine. GIOVANNI brings her credit card and she signs the slip.

GIOVANNI: Did you enjoy the meal?

AMMY: Yeah, it was great.

GIOVANNI: Glad to hear it.

AMMY: You're the owner?

GIOVANNI: Ay.

AMMY: Had the restaurant long?

GIOVANNI: Been in the family for years.

AMMY: So you're from Edinburgh?

GIOVANNI: Ay.

AMMY: I love coming here.

GIOVANNI: You up for the Festival?

AMMY: I'm here to give a talk.

GIOVANNI: Oh yes?

AMMY: About the way the Third World is portrayed in the media.

GIOVANNI: Thought mebbe you were a journalist.

AMMY: No. (*Handing him a leaflet.*) Here, you could come. It's open to the public.

GIOVANNI: That's a sad photo.

AMMY: Actually the man who took it is from Edinburgh.

GIOVANNI: Is that so?

AMMY: You know him?

GIOVANNI: I think you know I do.

AMMY: Sorry?

GIOVANNI: Look young lady, what you after?

AMMY: I'm doing something about Stewart's work.

GIOVANNI: Well, I don't think there's anything I could tell you.

AMMY: I'm trying to understand some things about his background.

GIOVANNI: I see.

AMMY: Of course I've found out a lot already. And I know all about his parents dying.

GIOVANNI: Oh, you know about that?

AMMY: Oh yeah.

GIOVANNI: Well, there's not a lot more to tell.

AMMY: Did he talk much about his home life?

GIOVANNI: No.

AMMY: What never?

GIOVANNI: It was very obvious that he didna want to. When you're that age you're very sensitive about things like that. So I didna push it.

AMMY: You never went to his house?

GIOVANNI: Stewart never invited me. Later, afterwards, I understood why.

AMMY: Of course. Yeah. It was so tragic, wasn't it?

(*GIOVANNI doesn't respond.*)

So you didn't meet his family?

GIOVANNI: Look, young lady, you speak to Stewart. I'm not the man to tell you anything about the McNulty's that you don't know already.

(*AMMY cannot conceal her excitement that he has told her the surname.*)

I think you'd better go.

AMMY: I just want to understand why he became a photojournalist. (*Indicating the leaflet.*) You know? His photos are so dark and full of suffering. They had a big impact on my life actually.

GIOVANNI: I'm closing. I'm sorry.

AMMY: Well, if you do remember anything that might be relevant.

(*She hands him her card.*)

GIOVANNI: I don't think I will.

(*He doesn't take it.*)

AMMY: Nice meeting you. Great meal.

GIOVANNI: Thank you.

(*She goes. He takes off his tie and starts to change.*
KATE comes and puts her arms around him. They lie on the floor. THEN.)

KATE: Just think.

GIOVANNI: What?

KATE: People will be sitting here eating their spaghetti bolognaise in a few hours.

GIOVANNI: Ay.

KATE: Little will they know.

GIOVANNI: Just as well. They'd be on to the health inspector.

(*She laughs.*)

(*Mimicking a Morningside lady.*) Oooh, Donald, I don't know what's in this cream sauce but it's very tasty.

KATE: You're gross.

(*They kiss.*)

You'd think if something really important happened in a place then you'd be able to feel it. You should be able to.

GIOVANNI: In one of my Dad's flats the tenant killed his wife. Blood everywhere. We had to have the whole place redecorated. It was empty for years.

KATE: That's horrible.

GIOVANNI: Ay.

KATE: I was talking about somewhere where something nice had happened.

GIOVANNI: I know.

KATE: I'd like to think that there'll always be a little bit of us here.

GIOVANNI: Like a stain on the carpet?

(*She hits him.*)

There will be. For me there will be. Every time I walk past here with somebody's pizza I'll get a hard on.

KATE: Can you not be romantic for one minute?

GIOVANNI: How about this?

(*He kisses her.*)

KATE: I'll have to go soon.

GIOVANNI: Can I see you tomorrow?

KATE: I don't know.

(*He is hurt.*)

It isna easy.

GIOVANNI: You're nearly sixteen.

(*They hold each other.*)

And I won't be able to see you in the summer.

KATE: What?

GIOVANNI: I've got to go t'Italy.

KATE: Why?

GIOVANNI: My Dad wants me to work in my uncle's restaurant in Naples. Get some experience there.

(*She says nothing. She puts on her clothes.*)

Kate.

KATE: What?

GIOVANNI: It's just for the summer.

KATE: (*Turning on him.*) I thought you cared about me!

GIOVANNI: I do.

KATE: So much that you can leave me for the whole summer.

(*Pause.*)

GIOVANNI: I don't want to go.

KATE: Why are you then?

GIOVANNI: Look, I'll talk to my Dad. Mebbe I can persuade him I don't need to.

KATE: Do what you like. Don't worry about me.

GIOVANNI: Don't be like that.

KATE: Like what?

GIOVANNI: So cold. It frightens me.

KATE: I've got to go.

GIOVANNI: Are you going down to see Stewart off on Saturday?

KATE: Maybe.

GIOVANNI: I'll see you then.

KATE: I don't know.

GIOVANNI: I'll speak to my Dad.

(*She goes. He is close to tears. She returns suddenly and kisses him passionately.*)

KATE: Don't let me be like that.

GIOVANNI: What?

KATE: Cold. I don't want to be cold.

GIOVANNI: I won't.

(*She goes. GIOVANNI finishes changing.*)

Scene 17

STEWART is standing with his kit bag. THEN.
KATE enters.

KATE: All set?

STEWART: Yeah.

(*Pause.*)

Uncle Jack's late.

KATE: Mmmm.

STEWART: You coming with us to Leith?

KATE: I don't know.

(*LIZ enters.*)

STEWART: You not even going to say goodbye to me?

(*LIZ doesn't respond.*)

KATE: Liz.

(*STEWART reaches out to touch LIZ. She slaps his hand away.*)

(*Hitting LIZ.*) Don't.

LIZ: Aowh.

KATE: Wee brat!

LIZ: That hurt.

KATE: Serves you right.

STEWART: Leave her.

(*MARGARET enters.*)

MARGARET: (*To LIZ.*) Have you done your messages this morning? There's no tea in the house.

STEWART: We're waiting for Uncle Jack to give me a lift.

MARGARET: (*Ignoring him.*) If you break your routine one day, you'll be breaking it the next. Before you know it there'll be chaos reigning in the house.

LIZ: I want to go to Leith with them.

MARGARET: You'll get out on those steps, my lady. And make sure there's not a speck of dirt on them. And afterwards you can run down the shop and get some tea. You hear me?

LIZ: Yes.

(*ANDREW enters.*)

MARGARET: Look at the state of you.

ANDREW: Nobody brought me any tea this morning.

MARGARET: You'll get your tea.

KATE: I'll get some on my way back from Leith.

ANDREW: You going to Leith?

STEWART: I'm going on board this morning.

ANDREW: Ah, so you are. So you are.

(*He looks at MARGARET.*
Knock at the door.)

KATE: (*Going.*) That'll be Uncle Jack.

ANDREW: Well, look after yourself.

STEWART: I will.

MARGARET: You had your wash?

ANDREW: Not yet.

MARGARET: I've switched the immersion off.

ANDREW: Right.

(*KATE enters with JACK.*)

JACK: Good morning.

MARGARET: (*Ignoring him. To ANDREW.*) Well go on, the water will be getting cold.

ANDREW: I'm just up, Jack. Havena had my wash.

JACK: Right you are. You all set?

STEWART: Yes.

JACK: I see you've used my kit bag.

    (*KATE picks up STEWART's kit bag.*)

MARGARET: (*To KATE.*) There's the washing to be done.

JACK: For Christ's sake her brother's going away the day.

MARGARET: I'll thank you not to blaspheme in this house.

KATE: I'll do the washing when I get home.

JACK: Right, come on.

STEWART: Bye, Lizzie.

    (*LIZ hurls herself at him to hug him.*)

LIZ: I don't want you to go.

STEWART: I know.

MARGARET: (*To LIZ.*) I thought I told you to do your chores.

    (*LIZ goes.*)

STEWART: Bye, Dad.

ANDREW: (*Avoiding his eye.*) Ay.

STEWART: (*To MARGARET.*) Bye.

    (*She doesn't respond.*

    JACK, STEWART and KATE go. ANDREW stays looking
    at MARGARET.)

MARGARET: Go on!

    (*ANDREW goes. MARGARET sits. She is shaking. ANDREW*
    is in the bathroom.

    LIZ enters with some tea.)

LIZ: I found some at the back of the cupboard.

    (*MARGARET tastes it.*)

MARGARET: (*Throwing it at LIZ.*) Ugh. That's that Chinese
    muck. You stupid girl.

    (*LIZ is holding her scalded arm.*)

    Away and run it under the tap.

Scene 18

The docks. GIOVANNI, STEWART, KATE and JACK. THEN.

JACK: I told my pal Ronnie to keep an eye on you.

STEWART: Thanks, Uncle Jack.

JACK: You'll have a great time. Wish I was coming with you.

STEWART: (*To GIOVANNI.*) This was supposed to be me and you doing this together.

JACK: It's not too late. They need more hands in the galley.

GIOVANNI: I can't I've got to go t'Italy.

JACK: Italy? Very nice.

STEWART: When?

GIOVANNI: Next week.

(*STEWART looks at KATE.*)

JACK: Well, laddie…

STEWART: Yeah. Bye then.

JACK: Don't worry about Katie here. I'll look after her. Won't I, Kate?

(*He puts his arm around her.*)

KATE: Bye.

STEWART: Bye.

KATE: Go on.

(*STEWART and JACK go.*)

GIOVANNI: I'll write to you.

KATE: Don't bother.

GIOVANNI: Kate. Please.

(*JACK returns.*)

JACK: That's the last we'll see of him for a while.

KATE: He'll be back at Christmas.

JACK: I wouldna bet on it. He'll be sunning himself in foreign parts. Lucky devil.

(*KATE shivers.*)

You cold?

KATE: No.

JACK: Fancy a wee drink in the pub to warm you up?

KATE: Okay.

JACK: (*To GIOVANNI.*) Can we give you a lift anywhere?

GIOVANNI: I've my bike.

JACK: Oh well. See you then.

GIOVANNI: Yes.

(*JACK and KATE start to go.*)

Bye Kate.

KATE: Bye.

(*JACK and KATE go. GIOVANNI watches them.
MARGARET is bandaging LIZ's hand. THEN.*)

LIZ: It hurts.

MARGARET: Don't be such a baby.
(*Singing quietly over the next scene.*) 'The second wee craw
Fell and broke his jaw' etc.
(*STEWART and LUIS on board a ship. NOW.*)

STEWART: You feeling better?

LUIS: No.

STEWART: I was sick as a dog on my first voyage.

LUIS: Are we nearly there?

STEWART: We'll be going into the Firth of Forth soon. Way
over there that's Fife and on that side, that's North
Berwick. I used to go there when I was a kid.

LUIS: With Liz?

STEWART: Yes.

LUIS: Will we see her today?

STEWART: She doesn't live in Edinburgh any more.

LUIS: I thought we come to see her.

STEWART: That's not what I said.

LUIS: Why we fucking come here then?
(*ANDREW is sitting shivering in the bath. LIZ is curled up
with MARGARET. It is a rare moment of tenderness between
them. THEN.*)

MARGARET: You'll soon be all I've got left. And then one
day, you'll leave too.

LIZ: I won't.

MARGARET: You will. Then I'll be left on m'own in this
house with your father and ma life will have ended.
I won't be any use to anybody.

LIZ: I won't leave you.

MARGARET: You go out to the shop and I'm thinking
already that you won't come back.

LIZ: I always do.

MARGARET: I'd be better off dead than left in this house
on my own with your father.
(*JACK and KATE in the pub. THEN.*)

JACK: Cheers.

KATE: Cheers.

JACK: We willnae tell your mother that you've been in the pub drinking.

(*KATE giggles.*)

Although I'm sure you get up to much worse things.

KATE: Like what?

JACK: Oooh, let me see...

KATE: What?

JACK: Well like letting boys take liberties.

KATE: I don't know what you're talking about Uncle Jack.

JACK: Do you not?

KATE: No! What do you mean?

JACK: Well, you see, they start off stroking your leg, like this.

(*He strokes her leg.*)

KATE: Oh yeah?

JACK: Yeah. And then their hand goes higher.

(*He lets his hand go higher.*)

KATE: What happens then, Uncle Jack?

JACK: I'll need to show you properly.

(*Pause.*)

I should be taking you home.

KATE: Just one more drink.

JACK: You sure?

KATE: Ay.

JACK: Okay then.

(*MARGARET and LIZ. THEN.*)

MARGARET: You don't really like school, do you?

LIZ: I don't know.

MARGARET: From what I can see they don't teach you anything worth knowing.

LIZ: I like Miss MacKintosh.

MARGARET: Oh well, if you prefer your teacher to your mother.

LIZ: I didn't say that.

MARGARET: You're just like the rest of them. Not a thought for your poor mother. I might as well be dead, then you'd all be happy.

LIZ: I don't want you to die.

MARGARET: The sooner the better. You'll have me out of the way and you'll be able to forget about me.

LIZ: I won't. I won't.

MARGARET: When you go out I'm worried sick.

LIZ: Why?

MARGARET: That wee boy from Glasgow! He went down the shop to buy some sweeties. They never found out what happened to him. Someone saw him getting into a blue car but it was never traced.

LIZ: I'll stay with you.

MARGARET: You don't want to.

LIZ: I do.

(*KATE and JACK. JACK returns with more drinks. THEN.*)

KATE: What's it like at the races?

JACK: Musselburgh?

KATE: Ay.

JACK: It's great. The excitement of it all, you know? Even if you dinnae win.

KATE: Will you take me?

JACK: You want me to?

KATE: Yes.

JACK: We understand each other pretty well, you and me.

KATE: Yes.

JACK: You wanna go for a wee drive wi me before we go home? We can always say the car broke down.

KATE: What for?

JACK: Thought you might like a drive to the Firth wi me.

KATE: What to do?

JACK: To look.

KATE: Okay then.

(*MARGARET is stroking LIZ's hair and humming the tune of 'Three Wee Craws'. THEN.*
LUIS and STEWART on the boat. NOW.)

STEWART: Look, there's the Bridge.

(*LUIS doesn't look.*)

God! You're a fucking pleasure to be with, aren't you?

(AMMY on her mobile.)

AMMY: Alan, it's Ammy on Sunday. Hope you're having a nice romantic time in Paris with your wife. I've got a name for you. It's McNulty. Capital M, small c, capital N, u, l, t, y. I think. I couldn't find anything on the net so I wondered if you could check it out. I'm in Edinburgh – I've got my talk in the morning but I'll stay up here and see what more I can dig up. So ring me when you get back. We're closing in on him. Bye!

LUIS: Stewart.

STEWART: What?

LUIS: Are you going to make me go back to Brazil?

STEWART: You might have to.

LUIS: You loved my mother?

STEWART: What?

LUIS: She say she never knew if you love her.

STEWART: Course I did.

LUIS: So why you leave her?

STEWART: I was young.

LUIS: She always keep your photo. Even after she marry Fernando.

(STEWART doesn't respond.)

I like it here with you. You let me stay.

STEWART: We'll see.

LUIS: You promise?

STEWART: Look. You can see the Castle.

LUIS: You promise?

STEWART: Ay, I promise.

(They watch Edinburgh get closer.
JACK is kissing KATE with his hand up her skirt. THEN.
ANDREW sits in the bath with his hands over his ears. THEN.
GIOVANNI takes a photo from his wallet and looks at it. THEN/NOW.
MARGARET strokes LIZ's hair and hums 'Three Wee Craws'. THEN.
AMMY prepares for her talk. NOW.)

End of First Half.

Scene 19

AMMY giving her speech. NOW.

AMMY: Before we go any further, I'd like to ask you
something. How many of you have actually been to the
Third World? Just by a show of hands. How many of
you have been to India or one of the poorer countries
in Asia? Right, thank you. And what about Africa?
I see. Thanks. And South America? Right. Right, thank
you. And of those people who have put up their hands,
how many of you have been to those countries as part
of your jobs? I see. Thank you. And how many of you
went to one of those places to travel or for a holiday?
Right. Interesting. Thanks. I see that I'm addressing a
well-travelled and well-informed audience.
(*She smiles at them.*)
Could we have the slide back up, please?
(*A slide of an African woman holding an emaciated baby.*)
To return to Stewart Reid's photo. It's trying to shock
us out of our complacency. The photographer and
publisher want us to do something about the famine
which has caused this. I'm sure we'd all applaud
these aims. However the photo appears in a magazine
surrounded by all the trappings of consumerism, among
articles on style and foreign travel. A magazine that we
buy to read on our day off, in the comfort of our
homes, surrounded by our families, with the aroma of
Sunday dinner floating in from the kitchen. Which is
only fitting because the photo itself is a consumer
article. It was published in order to sell copies of the
magazine in question. We might find this a bit ironic.
Maybe even a bit voyeuristic.
(*She stares at the audience.*)
And what about the photographer? He claims to be an
idealist. And yet I detect in all photojournalists a certain
vanity about their work, a certain macho posturing about
the dangers to which they expose themselves. Stewart
Reid prides himself on his style. He rejects the tele-photo

lens and likes to put himself right in the middle of the action. You might think that he enjoys the danger and the horrors that he captures with his camera. Why is this I wonder?

(*She stares at the audience again.*)

The Third World represents for the westerner a realm that is explored and exploited not just for raw material and labour but also for experience. Technological advances protect the Western Man and Woman more and more from the natural world and so they turn to the undeveloped countries for adventure, for the opportunity to journey to "the heart of darkness," for an encounter with "The Horror." And afterwards they return to their comfortable lives reassured and triumphant that they have passed the test. Have you people who have worked and travelled and holidayed in the Third World not felt this obscene sense of achievement on your return?

(*She eyeballs the audience.*)

And then there are the bold journalists who go to the very core of the danger and emerge with their reports and their photos. How we admire them. How we shudder at the images of suffering they deliver up to us. I'm not saying altruism doesn't exist. But the wallowing in misery that photos such as this encourage does not shake us out of our complacency. Far from it! It reassures us. (*Pointing to the slide.*) She helps us to feel invincible. Through her we can avoid our own failures, our own inadequacies, our own pain. Our own darkness. How grateful we are to the brave photojournalist. We shower him with praise and awards. He reminds us that we Westerners live in the light. It is people from the Third World, particularly the dark continent itself, who languish in eternal night. Thank you.

(*Applause. AMMY gathers together her notes. STEWART approaches her.*)

STEWART: Well!

AMMY: Oh!

STEWART: Hi.

AMMY: I didn't –

STEWART: I was in Edinburgh. Saw it advertised.

AMMY: Right.

STEWART: You're quite a speaker.

AMMY: Thanks.

STEWART: I wondered what you were going to say next. I thought mebbe you'd tell them how big my dick was.

AMMY: I wouldn't want to embarrass you.

STEWART: Correct me if I'm wrong here, but didn't you say you admired my work? Didn't I inspire you to become a journalist? Have I got that wrong?

AMMY: No.

STEWART: I'm glad I'm not someone whose work you despise then.

AMMY: I'm just tired of seeing my race portrayed as victims.

STEWART: (*Pointing to the audience.*) I should think they're feeling pretty victimised at the moment. I know I am. Nice of you to ask me if you could use my photo by the way. Very ethical.

AMMY: I'm sorry.

STEWART: You fucking should be.

AMMY: Did you ask her?

STEWART: What?

AMMY: Did you ask her if you could take it?

STEWART: Ahhh. I've met people like you before, darling.

AMMY: I'm not your darling.

STEWART: People who use ideology to settle scores. Pretend to be morally superior when all they're doing is getting their own back. Aren't you ashamed of what you just did to them? (*Pointing at the audience.*).

AMMY: Making them think?

STEWART: Using the colour of your skin to make them sit up and pay attention and then throwing it back in their face and making them feel guilty.

AMMY: Maybe I'm just doing it to get another rung up the ladder.

STEWART: You don't know anything about those people. Arrogant, smug little shit. What's the darkness in your heart? That's what I'd like to know. What's your pain that makes you do that to people, I wonder?

(*He goes.*

AMMY gathers her papers together. She is very upset and wipes her eyes. Suddenly she sees LUIS standing watching her.)

AMMY: Hi.

LUIS: Hi.

AMMY: I didn't see you.

(*LUIS nods.*)

You listen to my talk?

LUIS: No. I was outside.

AMMY: Right.

LUIS: Are you still writing your article about Stewart?

AMMY: I am.

(*Pause.*)

LUIS: You won't tell him, will you?

AMMY: What?

LUIS: That I gave you that address.

AMMY: Of course not.

(*She gathers together her papers.*)

LUIS: Why you not married?

AMMY: Pardon.

LUIS: You very beautiful.

AMMY: Thank you.

LUIS: So why?

AMMY: I was.

LUIS: Yeah? What happen?

AMMY: Things didn't work out.

LUIS: He was a violent man?

AMMY: No.

LUIS: In Brazil are many violent men. They beat wives. They beat child. They don't care. Sometimes they kill.

AMMY: That happens in England too.

(*He leans close to her. She senses his need for comfort.*)

LUIS: So why you leave him?

AMMY: We wanted different things.

LUIS: You wanted career. I understand this. So you have boyfriend?

AMMY: You're very nosy.

LUIS: Do you?

AMMY: No, not really.

LUIS: You have a kinda boyfriend.

AMMY: Yes.

LUIS: This is like Stewart. He only ever have kinda
girlfriends. In London he has a different girl every night.

AMMY: Really?

LUIS: My mother she said he never let anyone close to him.

AMMY: No?

LUIS: Many men do this.

AMMY: Do you miss your mother?

(*LUIS shrugs.*)

LUIS: You don't want children?

AMMY: Pardon?

LUIS: You don't like?

AMMY: Yes.

LUIS: So why you don't have?

AMMY: I do. I've got a little girl.

LUIS: Where she?

AMMY: She lives with my mother when I'm away.

(*He looks at her.*)

LUIS: You and Stewart. You the same.

AMMY: How?

LUIS: He have only his work. Nothing else.

AMMY: Yes?

LUIS: He have sister but he don't know where she is.

AMMY: What's her name?

LUIS: Liz. This is a name?

AMMY: It is. Where does she live?

LUIS: I don't know.

(*Pause.*)

He don't have anyone.

AMMY: He's got you.

(*LUIS shrugs again.*)

LUIS: We go away from Edinburgh now. He take me to
Loch Lomond.

AMMY: Oh.

LUIS: You want to come?

AMMY: I can't, Luis.

LUIS: You been there already?

AMMY: No, but –

LUIS: So come.

AMMY: I don't think Stewart would want me to.

LUIS: Please. When Stewart and me are together we say nothing. It is horrible. He get drunk and he don't say nothing and we always quarrel. If you come maybe he don't get so drunk.

(*STEWART enters.*)

STEWART: There you are. I've been looking for you everywhere.

LUIS: I was here!

STEWART: I hope you haven't been hustling.

(*LUIS looks at AMMY.*)

AMMY: He hasn't.

STEWART: Come on then.

(*LUIS gets up to go. He looks at AMMY pleadingly.*)

AMMY: Stewart?

STEWART: Yes.

AMMY: I'm sorry about the lecture.

(*STEWART doesn't reply.*)

You're right, I was trying to get my own back. For Southwold.

STEWART: I know. I'm sorry.

AMMY: Can we start again?

(*Pause.*)

STEWART: You like to go for a coffee?

AMMY: Okay.

STEWART: Right. There's a place just –

AMMY: Yes.

STEWART: Right.

(*They turn to go. AMMY winks at LUIS.*)

Scene 20

KATE and JACK at the racecourse at Musselburgh. THEN.

KATE: Come on! Come on, Maxwelton Braes! Yes. He's winning! Yes! Yes! We've won.
(*She throws her arms around JACK.*)
JACK: Thirty-five pounds.
(*She kisses him.*)
I can pick the fillies, can't I?
KATE: Can you?
JACK: Ay.
KATE: What about Aunty Eileen? You picked her?
JACK: Don't be like that.
KATE: Like what?
JACK: You know I'd do anything for you, Katy.
KATE: Would you?
JACK: One day, when I've got enough money, we'll take off. We'll just go and not tell anybody where we've gone.
KATE: Where will we go?
JACK: Anywhere you fancy. Australia! What about Australia? That's the place to go for a new life.
KATE: What would we do?
JACK: I fancy running a bar somewhere. Bondi Beach.
KATE: Do they have horse-racing in Australia?
JACK: Have you not heard of the Melbourne Cup? Better climate there too. What do you think? Eh?
KATE: What about Liz?
JACK: What about her?
KATE: We'd have to take her. We couldn't leave her here on her own.
JACK: No. I suppose not. Better get our winnings.
(*He goes.*
MARGARET at home. THEN.)
MARGARET: Liz! Liz! Where's your father's tea?
(*LIZ goes to her with the tea cup.*)
Give it here.
(*She takes a bottle of pills from her bag and puts two in the tea.*)
Give it a good stir.

(*LIZ stirs the tea.*

KATE leaves JACK and enters the house.)

What time do you call this?

KATE: I had to stay late. We had extra English.

MARGARET: I'm not having you walking the streets after dark. (*To LIZ.*) Let's see.

(*LIZ shows her the tea.*)

Make sure they've dissolved.

KATE: Those pills just make him more depressed.

MARGARET: Who's asking you? Are you a doctor?

KATE: They're not even his prescription.

MARGARET: Are you a doctor?

(*KATE doesn't respond.*)

You want him keeping us awake half the night? Is that what you want?

KATE: They were asking about her at school again this morning.

MARGARET: What did you say?

KATE: What you told me to say. That she's staying with Aunty Hilda in England. They wanted to know what school she's going to.

(*MARGARET doesn't respond.*)

They'll send somebody round.

MARGARET: (*To LIZ.*) Take your father up his tea.

(*LIZ goes.*)

You're not coming in here upsetting her.

KATE: They'll check up.

MARGARET: I need her home here to help look after your father. Do you want to stay home and look after him? Because you can!

KATE: She should be going to school.

MARGARET: Get down on your knees!

KATE: I'm just saying –

MARGARET: Get down on your knees.

(*KATE kneels.*)

Beg the Lord for forgiveness for the way you talk back to me.

(*Upstairs, LIZ is watching her father drink his tea.*)

ANDREW: What?

LIZ: Nothing.

(He finishes the tea and turns the cup over in the saucer.
LIZ moves in.)

ANDREW: There was a man with a dog in here yesterday.
A wizened old man and a black poodle. I thought it was
the devil coming after me.

(He continues to read the leaves.)

In the hospital they used tea bags. There was this old
man. Every day he got frantic because there were no
leaves in the tea-cup. He thought the future was going to
be blank, you see?

(He laughs.)

He was mad. I'm no mad, you know, darling.

LIZ: I know.

ANDREW: If I could just get rid of these voices.

(LIZ looks at him.)

ANDREW: What sort of life is it, eh?

(He yawns.)

Ah, never mind. With any luck it'll soon be over.

(He yawns again.
He is suddenly asleep. LIZ takes the cup and creeps away.)

Scene 21

The nursing home. GIOVANNI is looking at the bird, feeling its
wing. NOW.
LIZ enters with a cup of tea.

LIZ: There you are.

GIOVANNI: Thank you. Are you not having one?

LIZ: I've already had my tea.

GIOVANNI: He's getting better. He'll soon be able to fly.

LIZ: I worry about the cat.

GIOVANNI: Mmmm.

(He drinks his tea.)

Liz. Do you think sometimes about Stewart?

(She doesn't reply.)

Do you not wonder whether mebbe you should get in contact with him?

(*She starts to feed the bird.*)

Donna said he writes to you.

LIZ: He used to.

GIOVANNI: When you were in that children's home?

LIZ: Yes.

GIOVANNI: What about when you were living in the hostel in Glasgow?

(*She nods.*)

You don't ever feel like replying?

LIZ: Has he been in contact with you?

GIOVANNI: No.

(*He watches her.*)

Does he have your address in here?

LIZ: I don't want him to have it.

(*LIZ continues feeding the bird.*)

GIOVANNI: Mebbe Donna would like to meet him one day.

LIZ: No.

GIOVANNI: In her last letter she says she's been thinking about you and the family over there in India.

LIZ: If Stewart really wanted to see me, he'd find me.

(*She starts to go.*)

GIOVANNI: Do you not want to read Donna's letter?

LIZ: I saw some snails over by the wall this morning. Blackbirds like snails don't they?

GIOVANNI: Yes they do.

(*She goes. GIOVANNI reads the letter.*
AMMY on her mobile. NOW.)

AMMY: Alan. I thought you'd be back by now. I'm in a toilet in a cafe so I hope I'm not breaking up. He's got a sister. Liz short for Elizabeth. See if you can track her down. Gotta go. Kiss, kiss. Ring me!

Scene 22

KATE is being sick in the bathroom. THEN.
KATE turns round to find MARGARET watching her.

MARGARET: What's wrong with you?

KATE: Nothing.

MARGARET: I heard you being sick yesterday morning.

KATE: It must have been something I ate.

MARGARET: And the morning before that.

KATE: It must be a bug.

(*LIZ goes to them. MARGARET holds up a packet of sanitary towels.*)

MARGARET: These have been in your room for months. You haven't used a single one.

KATE: I've got others.

MARGARET: You stupid girl.

KATE: What?

MARGARET: Whose is it?

(*KATE says nothing.*)

I'll find out. And when I do, someone will have to pay, I tell you that. You were underage. Someone's going to be in a lot of trouble.

(*KATE doesn't respond.*)

It was that Italian boy, wasn't it?

KATE: Who?

MARGARET: Don't play the innocent. Liz has told me all about you going to the fair with him.

KATE: Well, you're wrong. It wasna him.

MARGARET: Don't lie to me.

KATE: He's in Italy. He's been there for months now. He's not even in Edinburgh.

MARGARET: Who was it then?

KATE: It could have been an immaculate conception.

(*MARGARET slaps her.*)

MARGARET: You dirty little slut. If your grandfather was alive he'd beat you within an inch of your life.

KATE: He's not though, is he?

MARGARET: (*Screaming.*) Hold your tongue!

She takes out the key to the cellar.

(*To LIZ.*) Lock her downstairs.

KATE: For God's sake!

MARGARET: You'll stay down there until you tell me who's the father of that child. (*To LIZ.*) Go on!

KATE: You really want to know? Ask Uncle Jack.

MARGARET: Get down those stairs.

KATE: He's been taking me out in his car. We've been going to pubs. We've been drinking together. We've been going to the races. Putting money on the horses, gambling. Ask him who the father is.

MARGARET: (*Screaming.*) Get her out of my sight. (*To LIZ.*) Take her downstairs! Take her downstairs!

(*KATE and LIZ look at each other. KATE goes. LIZ follows. MARGARET takes a pill. She turns and ANDREW is standing there.*)

What are you doing out of bed?

ANDREW: Come to see what's going on.

MARGARET: There's nothing going on.

ANDREW: Ahhh.

MARGARET: Now get back to bed.

ANDREW: Stewart back yet?

MARGARET: Stewart?

ANDREW: Is he back from school?

MARGARET: He's in South America with his ship.

ANDREW: South America is it?

MARGARET: Go on!

ANDREW: Ay, with his ship.

(*He goes.*)

Scene 23

KATE: (*Off.*) Uncle Jack! Uncle Jack!

MARGARET: Get down on your knees and beg the Lord for forgiveness, Jack.

JACK: Margaret.

MARGARET: I know she led you on, Jack. I saw the way she was with you. You think I didn't see it when she lowered her head and looked at you sideways through her eyelashes and when she hitched up her skirt so that you could see her legs.

JACK: Let me speak to her. We'll get it sorted.

MARGARET: She has to repent, Jack. I'm doing it for her own good. Her heart is weighed down by deceit and carnality. She can only learn by admitting her sin and begging forgiveness from her maker. She needs solitude and quiet to do that. You have to do that too, Jack.

JACK: Where's the key? For God's sake, woman!

MARGARET: God? What do you know about God?

JACK: You canna keep her locked down there forever.

MARGARET: You've sinned, Jack. You've trod the path to temptation and damnation. It's like Daddy always said, you'll go to hell with your soul blackened by your wicked deeds. Please, Jack, pray with me.

JACK: You're mad, woman! Just like the old man.

MARGARET: If he was mad then it was you that made him like it with your wickedness and waywardness. "A girl in every port," wasn't that what you used to joke about just to make Daddy angry? And you used to laugh at us going to Church and praying for your salvation. We thought, Daddy thought, that when you settled down with Eileen things would change. But it didn't stop you, did it? You think we didn't hear about that girl over in Kirkaldy? And the one in the office at the shipyard? You think Eileen didn't know? It killed Daddy with grief to see you continue in your wicked way.

JACK: Huh!

MARGARET: And as if that wasn't enough you poisoned my own son's mind and led him down the same road.

JACK: He couldn't wait to get away from you.

MARGARET: I never thought I'd live to thank God for the fact that Daddy's not here anymore. This would kill him a second time. Get down on your knees, Jack, and pray with me.

JACK: I'm going to bash down that door and get her out of there.

MARGARET: If you do, Jack, I won't have any choice but to go to the police. I don't want to do it. But I'll have to, Jack. I can't let the two of you carry on in your wickedness.

JACK: Maggie, please. I beg you.

MARGARET: Don't beg me. Beg the Lord God for forgiveness.

JACK: I don't want any harm to come to her.

MARGARET: You should have thought of that when you were letting her lead you astray.

JACK: Can I no just talk to her?

MARGARET: She's no concern of yours anymore. Now pray with me or leave this house for good.

(*JACK looks at her.*)

Oh Lord God, help us in our hour of need. Wash us clean so that we may tread once more the path of goodness and light. Deliver us, Lord, from the temptations of the flesh that assault us daily.

(*JACK goes.*)

KATE: Uncle Jack? Uncle Jack?

MARGARET: Oh Lord, lead the wicked back to the ways of righteousness so that they may see and acknowledge the true nature of their sins.

KATE: Uncle Jack! Uncle Jack!

Scene 24

The shores of Loch Lomond. AMMY, STEWART and LUIS. NOW.

STEWART: That's Ben Lomond. You can walk to the top of that.

AMMY: Will we see the monster?

STEWART: That's Loch Ness.

AMMY: Oh yes. Smile!

(*She takes a photo of STEWART.*)

LUIS: Look at this AMMY.

AMMY: What is it?

LUIS: Is a dead fish.

(*STEWART crosses to them.*)

STEWART: Let's see.

LUIS: (*Holding it up.*) Ugh!

STEWART: Put it down.

LUIS: (*Throwing it in STEWART's face.*) Ugghhhh!

STEWART: Luis!

(*The other two laugh at him.*)

That was a fucking stupid thing to do.

AMMY: You alright?

(*She goes to him and looks in his eye.*)

LUIS: Ammy!

(*He holds up the fish.*)

AMMY: (*To LUIS.*) Just a moment. (*To STEWART.*) Look up.

(*He does so. AMMY tries to get the speck of sand out. LUIS watches.*)

LUIS: Ammy! Take a photo of me!

AMMY: In a minute. (*To STEWART.*) Okay?

STEWART: (*Blinking.*) Yes.

AMMY: You're crying.

(*She wipes his face.*)

LUIS: Ammy!

STEWART: Be quiet for fuck sake.

LUIS: You be quiet!

STEWART: You hear yourself all the time? Ammy! Ammy! Look, Ammy!

AMMY: What do you want, Luis?

LUIS: Nothing.

AMMY: You want me to take a photo of you with the fish?

LUIS: No.

AMMY: Come on!

LUIS: I don't want you to.

AMMY: Oh Luis, come on.

LUIS: No.

(*He throws the fish away.*)

STEWART: Don't be such a baby, come on!

(*He goes and puts his arm around LUIS and poses. LUIS shakes him off.*)

LUIS: Get away from me!

AMMY: Luis, please.

LUIS: No. I told you.

STEWART: Don't talk to Ammy like that.

LUIS: I don't want my photo taken.

STEWART: There's that four year old again. Now come and apologise to Ammy.

AMMY: It's okay.

STEWART: He can just apologise.

LUIS: Fuck off.

STEWART: You quit swearing.

LUIS: *Porra!*

STEWART: I told you to quit swearing.

LUIS: You fucking swear all the fucking time. *Va tomor no cu! Filho da puta! Eu te queimo, viado fresco! Eu te fodo, fai daqui!*

(*STEWART approaches LUIS and hits him.*)

STEWART: Stop it!

AMMY: Stewart!

(*LUIS looks at STEWART for a moment and runs away.*)

STEWART: Little sod!

AMMY: Luis!

STEWART: Leave him! He's just fucking impossible.

AMMY: It can't be easy.

STEWART: It isn't, I can tell you.

(*He is burying the fish with his foot.*)

AMMY: I meant for him.

STEWART: What?

AMMY: Losing his mother. Coming over here.

STEWART: He can go back any time he wants.

AMMY: Has he got family in Brazil?

STEWART: Stepfather.

AMMY: How does he get on with him?

(*STEWART shrugs.*)

I think he probably beats him.

STEWART: What the fuck do you know?

AMMY: It was just something he said.

STEWART: You going to start telling me how to treat my son now?

AMMY: No.

STEWART: Good.

(*A mobile rings. They both look for their phones.*
STEWART pats his pocket. AMMY searches for her mobile.

STEWART finds his and realises it isn't ringing.
AMMY finds hers.)

AMMY: Hello.

Oh, hi.

Um, can I phone you back?

Really?

Yes, very interesting. Um –

Right, well –

Look, Alan, I can't talk now.

No, it's just not a good time.

Yes I will.

Of course.

Yeah, and you.

(*She hangs up.*)

Sorry.

(*Suddenly STEWART gets up.*)

STEWART: Luis! Luis!

(*He goes. AMMY follows.*)

Scene 25

KATE in the cellar. LIZ outside the door. THEN.

LIZ: Kate!

(*No response.*)

Kate!

KATE: What?

LIZ: She said she might let you out next week.

KATE: She said that last week.

LIZ: I think she meant it this time.

KATE: And the week before. And the week before that.

(*Pause.*)

I felt it kick this morning. You can feel it shifting around and getting comfy.

LIZ: I wish I could feel it.

(*Pause.*)

I thought of another name last night. For if it's a boy.

KATE: What?

LIZ: Donald.

KATE: I'm not calling it Donald.

LIZ: Why not?

KATE: Donald where's your trewsers!

(*Pause.*)

Liz!

LIZ: What?

KATE: You've got to get me out of here.

LIZ: I can't.

KATE: She's not giving me enough to eat. I'm supposed to eat healthy things so the baby will be strong and grow properly.

LIZ: You said you could feel it.

KATE: I can but it needs vitamins and things. Fruit.

LIZ: I could get a straw and give you orange juice to drink through the keyhole.

KATE: Where will you get orange juice?

(*Pause.*)

LIZ: She'll let you out if you ask Jesus for forgiveness.

KATE: I did. I got down on my knees and did it for her.

LIZ: She didn't believe you. You have to really repent. If you hadn't done bad things then she wouldn't be doing this.

KATE: For Christ's sake!

LIZ: Do not take the Lord's name in vain.

KATE: Oh, shut up!

LIZ: She said you brought it on yourself. That only bad girls do what you did with Uncle Jack. She said you have to reflect on your badness, otherwise you'll end up on the streets.

KATE: Bloody cow!

LIZ: Don't call her that!

KATE: Oh, piss off!

LIZ: You shouldn't swear.

(*Pause.*)

KATE: The baby will die if I stay in here. Do you want the baby to die?

LIZ: No.

KATE: Wouldn't you like to have a wee baby to look after? Just think! It would be ours and we could take care of it. I'd let you give it its bottle and we'd get wee clothes for it to wear. And we'll teach it our songs. Every night we'll stand each side its bed and we'll sing it to sleep and watch its little eyes close.

LIZ: Can he sleep in the room with us?

KATE: Of course. But you'll have to get me out of here.

LIZ: If I do, you'll run away.

KATE: I willna. Did I no say I'd never leave you?

LIZ: You wouldn't need me anymore. You'll have the baby.

KATE: Liz, I won't leave you. Get me out!

LIZ: I can't.

(*She runs away.*)

KATE: Liz! Liz!

Scene 26

AMMY and STEWART can be heard calling LUIS.

STEWART: (*Off.*) Luis! Luis!

AMMY: (*Off.*) Luis! Luis!

(*STEWART and AMMY enter. They are looking at Ben Lomond.*)

Do you think he's gone up there?

STEWART: He might have. Luis! Fuck!

AMMY: He'll be alright.

STEWART: It's getting dark.

AMMY: You look up there. I'll sort us out a room at that hotel.

STEWART: You don't have to get back to Edinburgh?

AMMY: No.

STEWART: I appreciate this.

(*He kisses her.*)

AMMY: Go on.

(*He goes.*)

STEWART: (*Off.*) Luis! Luis!

Scene 27

KATE is having the baby and shouting. THEN.

MARGARET: Keep your voice down.
  (*KATE groans.*)
  Put your hand over her mouth.
  (*LIZ puts her hand over KATE's mouth.*)
  Now push! But keep quiet!
  (*KATE groans.*)
  Yes, it hurts, doesn't it? These are the fruits of depravity.
  (*KATE groans.*)
  I thought I told you to cover her mouth.
  (*LIZ covers KATE's mouth.*
  The baby is born.
  JACK can be seen lighting a cigarette. ANDREW is sitting
  with his hands over his ears.
  Sound of baby crying.)

Scene 28

GIOVANNI is knocking at the door. MARGARET is playing Patience.
ANDREW is asleep in his chair. THEN.

MARGARET: Oh I thought it was my daughter. I thought
  she'd forgotten her key.
GIOVANNI: Mrs McNulty?
MARGARET: Yes.
GIOVANNI: I'm uh… Giovanni. I'm a friend of Stewart's.
MARGARET: Stewart's not here. He's away in the merchant
  navy.
GIOVANNI: Okay.
  (*She starts to go.*)
  Is it Kate who's away out?
MARGARET: No.
GIOVANNI: Oh right.
MARGARET: Kate's gone to England to live with my sister.
GIOVANNI: Oh.

MARGARET: Yes. She went for a visit and ended up staying. We think she's getting engaged.

GIOVANNI: Engaged?

MARGARET: Yes, to a very nice young man.

GIOVANNI: I see.

MARGARET: I'm sorry Stewart's not here.

GIOVANNI: It's okay.

MARGARET: Haven't even got an address for him. Sorry.

(*GIOVANNI goes.*

MARGARET returns to her Patience game. Baby cries.)

KATE: (*Off.*) Mother! Please! Bring her to me.

(*MARGARET carries on with her game.*)

(*Off.*) Liz! Mother!

ANDREW: Mmmm?

MARGARET: What?

ANDREW: What is it?

MARGARET: Go back to sleep.

(*He closes his eyes again.*)

KATE: (*Off.*) Mother!

(*LIZ enters. She gives MARGARET a bottle of pills.*)

MARGARET: What took you so long?

LIZ: I had to wait for him to make up the prescription.

MARGARET: He only had to count them and put them in the bottle.

LIZ: There were people waiting.

MARGARET: I thought you'd been kidnapped.

(*LIZ starts to go.*)

Where are you going?

LIZ: To pick the baby up.

MARGARET: You have to let them cry. If you pick them up every time they cry then they know they've got you just where they want you. Anyway...

LIZ: What?

MARGARET: You shouldn't get too attached to it.

LIZ: Why not?

MARGARET: You still haven't explained why you were so long. No-one saw you, did they?

LIZ: I met Mrs Goldstein.

MARGARET: I told you to come straight home.

LIZ: She asked me how Kate was enjoying England.

MARGARET: She didn't say anything about hearing the baby?

LIZ: No.

MARGARET: You must never tell anyone about this…

LIZ: Why not?

MARGARET: Because nobody must find out that it was ever here.

(*She starts counting the pills.*)

LIZ: But we are going to keep her, aren't we?

(*No response.*)

Mummy?

MARGARET: Shhhh!

LIZ: We are going to keep the baby.

MARGARET: Go on.

(*She carries on counting the pills. LIZ goes.*

LUIS sits on a ledge on Ben Lomond. In the distance STEWART and AMMY can be heard calling his name. LUIS has his hands over his ears. NOW.

LIZ is outside the cellar door. KATE is the other side of it. THEN.)

LIZ: I had to change her nappy three times the day. One of them was really dirty. Kate? Can you hear me?

KATE: Yes.

LIZ: And when I was changing her she did a pee and it went all over my hand. She did it on purpose.

KATE: How do you know?

LIZ: Because afterwards she smiled at me.

KATE: They don't know how to smile at that age.

LIZ: You didna see her. She smiled at me.

KATE: You should burp her. She might have wind.

LIZ: I know.

KATE: And when she sleeps make sure she's not too hot.

LIZ: You told me that.

KATE: But she mustn't get cold either.

LIZ: I know.

(*ANDREW gets up.*)

MARGARET: Where are you going?

ANDREW: My head's fuzzy.

(*He goes to where the baby is sleeping and looks at it.*)

KATE: Liz?

LIZ: What?

KATE: What's she gonnae do?

LIZ: I don't know.

KATE: I'm scared. For the baby. You know what she's like.

LIZ: I'm calling her Donna.

KATE: Okay.

LIZ: I'm glad she's a girl. We've still got things from when we were babies that she can wear. I found them in the chest on the landing. There's a wee pink dress with blue flowers.

KATE: She's not a doll, you know.

LIZ: I know.

KATE: Liz, you've got to do something.

LIZ: I've got to go now.

KATE: Liz!

(*LIZ goes.*

MARGARET is still playing Patience.

Baby cries. ANDREW moves towards it.

LIZ passes him and picks up the bundle.)

LIZ: What's wrong with you? You've got to keep quiet.

ANDREW: Stewart cried all night sometimes. Had terrible cholic. I used to sit up all night with him.

(*LIZ tries to give the baby its bottle.*)

LIZ: Daddy?

ANDREW: Ay?

LIZ: You won't let her do anything to the baby, will you?

ANDREW: (*Sings.*) 'The first wee craw

Was greetin for his maw

Greetin for his maw'

(*LIZ joins in.*)

LIZ/ANDREW: (*Sing.*) 'Greetin for his maw aw aw aw

The first wee craw was greetin for his maw

On a cold and frosty morning.'

(*MARGARET is standing at the doorway.*)

MARGARET: Andrew!

(He gets up. LIZ looks at him silently, pleading.)

Go on!

(He goes.)

I thought I told you not to get attached to it.

LIZ: I'm not.

(The baby starts crying again. ANDREW stops and looks back. MARGARET gets out her bottle of pills. She breaks one of the pills in half.)

MARGARET: Here.

LIZ: What?

MARGARET: Give it this.

LIZ: I'll get her quiet.

MARGARET: I don't want Mrs Goldstein coming and asking questions about a baby crying.

LIZ: Look, she's quiet now.

(The baby cries.)

Shhh.

MARGARET: Are you going to give it this?

LIZ: She doesn't need it.

MARGARET: Are you asking for solitude?

LIZ: No.

MARGARET: Then give it this.

(LIZ takes the pill.)

Put it in the bottle. Go on!

(LIZ does so.)

Shake it up.

(LIZ shakes the bottle.)

Now.

(LIZ looks at ANDREW. MARGARET turns.)

What are you doing standing there?

(ANDREW turns and goes.)

Give it the bottle.

(LIZ gives the baby the bottle. MARGARET watches.)

We can't keep it, you know.

LIZ: What are you going to do with her?

MARGARET: Never you mind.

(*MARGARET goes back to her Patience game. LIZ feeds the baby.*
LUIS and STEWART are sitting together on Ben Lomond.)

STEWART: You've still got that mark on your neck.

(*LUIS touches his neck.*)

That was from the umbilical cord. It was wrapped round your neck when you were born. Did your Mum tell you?

(*LUIS nods.*)

Never forget that night.

LUIS: You were there?

STEWART: Of course I was. Did your mother say I wasn't?

LUIS: I thought you left before.

STEWART: No. Pouring with rain it was. And we couldn't get a taxi to the hospital.

(*LUIS nods.*)

You weren't supposed to be born for another two months. In the end I carried your Mum into the street and stopped a car. Nearly got us both killed.

LUIS: All three.

STEWART: Ay, all three! Then when we got there and they realised you had the cord round your neck they had to get you out as quickly as possible. You were in an incubator for a week. I used to sleep there in the room with you to make sure you stayed alive.

(*Pause.*)

Ammy's waiting for us.

LUIS: Why did you do this?

STEWART: What?

LUIS: Stay with me?

STEWART: Well, your Mum was very weak, she could hardly move.

LUIS: But why you bother? In the end you went away.

(*He stands up and walks down the mountain. STEWART follows.*
ANDREW and MARGARET are both snoring. LIZ enters with two mugs of tea. THEN.)

> *The pills are on the table beside MARGARET. LIZ looks at them. She picks them up and unscrews the bottle. She puts a handful of pills in her hand. She pours them into one of the mugs. ANDREW opens his eyes. LIZ looks at the tea. She pours another handful of pills into MARGARET's mug.*
> *Suddenly she looks at ANDREW. She puts sugar in his tea and takes it to him. He grabs her arm and makes her pour the rest of the tablets in his tea. He begins to drink it.*
> *She returns the bottle to where she found it. She adds sugar to MARGARET's tea and stirs.*
> *MARGARET wakes up.*)

MARGARET: You'll wear a hole in that mug.

> (*LIZ gives her the tea.*)

Did you bring one for your father?

LIZ: Yes.

MARGARET: (*Reaching towards the pill bottle.*) You've forgotten his –

LIZ: I've already put them in.

MARGARET: How many?

LIZ: Two.

MARGARET: Should be enough.

> (*MARGARET sips her tea.*)

How many sugars did you put in this?

LIZ: Your usual.

> (*MARGARET and ANDREW sip their tea.*
> *LIZ runs away to GIOVANNI in the Nursing Home garden.*
> *NOW.*)

GIOVANNI: (*Handing her the letter.*) She wants you to come and live with us, Liz. You'd be doing us both a favour. She worries about me in that house on my own now that Maria's not there. And she wants you in her life. You belong with us.

LIZ: I can't.

GIOVANNI: Why not?

LIZ: I'm sick.

GIOVANNI: You're not sick. You never have been. No-one remembers, Liz. It's twenty years ago.

LIZ: You don't want someone like me living with you. Donna doesn't need that.

GIOVANNI: Donna loves you Liz. You're a good person.
(*LIZ cries.*
KATE goes to her parents. She holds a mirror under their noses. LIZ goes to her. THEN.)

LIZ: She was going to take the baby away. Remember what she did to the seagull?

KATE: It's okay.

LIZ: So I sent them to sleep. I sent her and Daddy to sleep. I wanted to make it so we could live here with the baby, just you and me.

KATE: I know.

LIZ: It was the only thing I could think of to do. So that we could stay here together. It'll be alright now. Won't it Kate? It was the right thing to do, wasn't it Kate? Kate? Wasn't it?

KATE: Help me.
(*They pick MARGARET up and drag her offstage.*
They return for ANDREW and take him off.
Sound of coal being shovelled.
AMMY and STEWART have just had a bath. She is combing his hair. NOW.)

STEWART: The coroner found coal dust in their lungs. And the flesh was worn off the bones on my mother's face before it rotted. He said that indicated that she'd been struggling when she died. Twisting her head from side to side, you know? Lacerating herself trying to get out. So it wasn't the drug that killed them. When Kate and Liz piled the coal over them they were still alive.

AMMY: Did Kate and Liz know that?

STEWART: At the inquest Kate said she knew and that Liz didn't. I don't know. Maybe she was trying to protect Liz. Take all the blame.
(*Pause.*)
I started having these nightmares lately.

AMMY: Yes?

STEWART: I can't think of anything worse can you? Knowing there's all this stuff on top of you and that you're not going to get out. No-one deserves that.

AMMY: No.

STEWART: So, those men in Afghanistan…it was a story close to my own heart.

AMMY: Yes.

STEWART: Haven't worked since then. No fucking point. Nothing I do has any fucking point.

AMMY: Stewart, Stewart. I'm sorry.

(*She cradles him.*

LIZ and KATE return covered in coal dust. They get into the bath and start washing each other. They sing 'Three Wee Craws' as before.)

Scene 29

AMMY in the bathroom with a towel around her. She is trying not to be overheard. NOW.

AMMY: Alan?

It's me.

Hi.

Yes, I'm sorry. I've been busy. I was out of Edinburgh. Loch Lomond.

No, I just wanted a little break.

Yes, on my own. Look, I don't think I want to pursue the Stewart Reid thing.

Well, there's not really much of a story.

You what? Oh right you've found that out.

No, I know about it. But I don't think –

Yes, I know about the sister too – well, both sisters.

(*LIZ enters the garden of the nursing home with a newspaper. She looks at the bird and sits down to read. NOW.*)

I just don't think we should be –

Because I don't. You what?

When?

Without even – ?

(*LIZ has found the article about the family.*)

I've told you I was at Loch Lomond.

So who's written the piece about the family?

You bastard!

I don't want my name on the byline. That's not what its about.
When's it appearing?
I see. Well I'll go out and buy a copy.
You fucking bastard.
(*She hangs up.*
LIZ is sitting with her hands over her ears rocking.)

Scene 30

The baby is crying. STEWART (with kitbag) goes to KATE holding the baby and stares at them. THEN.
LIZ enters with a benefit book.

LIZ: She's called Donna.
STEWART: Right.
LIZ: And she's very clever.
STEWART: I'm sure she is.
LIZ: Shall I get some more milk powder down the shop?
KATE: Okay.
LIZ: You havena signed the book.
STEWART: They left you the benefit book?
KATE: She knows I can do his signature. (*Signing the benefit book.*) Mummy said she'd write when Daddy was better.
STEWART: You havena got a telephone number for them?
LIZ: The hospital's down in the borders. They've got a special treatment they do there that Daddy needs.
      Haven't they, Kate?
KATE: Yes.
STEWART: Is it the one at Melrose?
KATE: I don't know.
STEWART: The two of you can't stay here on your own.
LIZ: Why not?
STEWART: Because you can't. You should be going to school for a start.
LIZ: I have to help look after the baby.
STEWART: You've got to go to school, Liz.
LIZ: We don't want you here. Go away!
STEWART: Don't be silly.

LIZ: I'm not silly. We don't need you. Go back to your ship.
(*She goes.*)

STEWART: Is it Giovanni's?
(*KATE says nothing.*)
Is it?

KATE: Who else's would it be?

STEWART: Does he know?

KATE: No.

STEWART: Should you not tell him?
(*KATE looks at the baby.*)
If he knew…

KATE: What?

STEWART: He'd want to help. He really likes you, you know.

KATE: He went away and he didn't come back for nearly a year.

STEWART: Why don't I go and talk to him?

KATE: It's too late.

STEWART: Of course it's not. Has Uncle Jack been round?

KATE: No.

STEWART: I'll go round and see him.

KATE: I don't want you to.

STEWART: Why not?

KATE: He doesn't know about the baby. I don't want him to find out.

STEWART: He's got to find out sometime.
(*Pause.*)
Kate.

KATE: What?

STEWART: Whose baby is it?

KATE: I thought we should have a fire the night.

STEWART: It's summer.

KATE: It'd be like Christmas in the old days. You weren't here for Christmas this year.

STEWART: The house does feel a bitty damp.

KATE: You could bring some coal up from the cellar.

STEWART: Okay then.

KATE: And we'll have the sherry she keeps in the kitchen cupboard.

(*He starts to go.*)

And then it's up to you.

STEWART: What?

KATE: What happens next.

(*He goes.*
Sound of coal being shovelled.
LIZ and KATE sip sherry. THEN.)

LIZ: It's nice this.

KATE: Ay.

LIZ: Can I give Donna some on my finger?

KATE: Go on then.

(*STEWART goes to them. He is shell shocked. His hands are black.*)

That's the trouble with coal.

LIZ: (*About DONNA.*) She doesna like it.

(*Pause.*)

KATE: I went out for my dinner…

LIZ: Oh yeah.

KATE: I went out for my dinner and I had a great big turkey.

LIZ: I went out for my dinner and I had a great big turkey with oatmeal stuffing.

(*They look at STEWART.*)

STEWART: Mmm?

LIZ: Go on.

STEWART: What?

LIZ: What did you have?

STEWART: I don't know.

KATE: Roast parsnips.

LIZ: Stewart went out for his dinner and he had a great big turkey with oatmeal stuffing and roast parsnips.

KATE: I went out for my dinner and I had a great big turkey with oatmeal stuffing, roast parsnips and bread sauce.

LIZ: I went out for my dinner and I had a great big turkey, oatmeal stuffing, roast parsnips, bread sauce and roast potatoes.

(*They look at STEWART. He gets up.*)

Where are you going?

STEWART: Down to the phone box.

(*He looks for money in his pocket.*)

KATE: You don't need money.

LIZ: Why not? Who are you phoning?

STEWART: Won't be long.

(*He goes.*)

LIZ: Who's he phoning?

Scene 31

JACK is watching television. STEWART stands before him. NOW.

JACK: I'm waiting for the racing. Got a few pennies on the horses.

(*STEWART nods.*)

STEWART: Do you still go to Musselburgh, Uncle Jack?

JACK: I don't get out so much lately.

(*He uses the remote control to change channels.*)

They're late with it.

(*Football on the other side. He turns the sound down.*)

You still got the flat in London?

STEWART: Yes.

JACK: Only the last letter was from Suffolk.

STEWART: I've got a house there.

JACK: You've done well for yourself.

STEWART: I'm okay.

JACK: Canna blame you.

STEWART: What?

JACK: For getting away like you did. Leaving it all behind.

(*He changes channels again.*)

STEWART: Looks like it's started.

JACK: No, that's Newmarket. I'm waiting for Ayr.

STEWART: Ah.

(*He changes channels.*)

JACK: Yes, it was no exactly easy living here afterwards.
Knowing that everybody was talking about the family.
It was hard. Eileen found it very hard. I sometimes think
it's what started getting her ill. She was never the same
again.

STEWART: I was sorry to hear about her.

JACK: Ay, she was a good woman.

(*He wipes his eye.*)

Of course you weren't to know.

STEWART: What?

JACK: When you went away the first time, you weren't to know what would happen. And it was a good life in the merchant navy there. I never wanted out. But of course when I married Eileen I had ma responsibilities. You can't always please yourself.

STEWART: You managed it.

JACK: What?

STEWART: You didn't exactly live the life of a saint when you came back.

JACK: Oh.

(*He coughs.*)

STEWART: I was wondering.

JACK: Ay?

STEWART: Do you know what happened to Liz?

JACK: She was in that children's home.

STEWART: I mean lately. The last time I heard from her she was in a hostel in Glasgow. But then she moved.

JACK: When was that?

STEWART: About five years ago. She left no forwarding address and my letters just come back.

JACK: And you her own brother! That's strange, isn't it?

STEWART: I tried to trace her. I thought she might need money.

JACK: She never even wrote to us. Not even a Christmas card.

STEWART: I see.

JACK: But I'm surprised she didn't want to keep in touch with you. I suppose she thought what with your work and your travelling you wouldna want to be continually minded of the past.

(*JACK switches over again to see if the racing has come on.*)

STEWART: Why didn't you ever do anything?

JACK: Eh?

STEWART: When we didn't have any food?

JACK: Food?

STEWART: When you saw the way she was with us.

JACK: I did my best.

STEWART: Did you get me the job on the Rio de Janeiro because you wanted me out of the way?

JACK: Why would I have wanted you out of the way, laddie?

(*JACK coughs. He spits in his handkerchief.*)

Liz keeps in contact with him.

STEWART: Who?

JACK: Your pal. Giovanni.

STEWART: Oh.

JACK: He'll have her address.

(*JACK coughs again.*)

STEWART: You should get that cough seen to.

JACK: I've had it ever since ma redundancy.

(*STEWART takes some money out of his wallet and gives it to JACK.*)

STEWART: Look after yourself.

JACK: I will.

(*STEWART starts to go.*)

It's best to let sleeping dogs lie, laddie.

(*STEWART looks at him.*)

That's what I told that journalist.

STEWART: What journalist?

JACK: The darkie woman. What was her name? Amy?

STEWART: She's been here?

JACK: Ay.

STEWART: When?

JACK: About a week ago. Did you no give her ma address?

STEWART: Ay, I must have.

JACK: Bye, lad.

STEWART: Bye.

(*He goes.*
JACK turns up the television.)

Scene 32

LUIS is sitting on the bed. STEWART is standing over him holding a newspaper.

STEWART: You little shit. This is how you repay me, huh? Selling information about me. I should never have brought you over here. I tell you one thing, you're getting on the first flight back to Rio. I never want to set eyes on you again. I hope Fernando beats the living daylights out of you.

(*AMMY has been listening.*)

AMMY: Stewart!

STEWART: You still here? I thought I told you to get out.

AMMY: Look, I didn't –

STEWART: "Oh Stewart, Stewart, I'm sorry, Stewart." Was any of it real?

AMMY: Of course it –

STEWART: First you pretend you're a great fan –

AMMY: I wasn't pret –

STEWART: – then you trash my work –

AMMY: I didn't trash –

STEWART: You pay this little shit to tell you things about me. You come up here tracking down my relations and my schoolfriends. You pretend you want to really get to know me –

AMMY: I did.

STEWART: Then you write this about me.

AMMY: Alan went behind my back.

STEWART: Oh, it was Alan was it? (*Quoting.*) "Ammy Richards examines the obsession with victims in the photos of Stewart Reid."

AMMY: I wrote that before.

STEWART: How would you like it? Huh? "The tragedy behind the lens. Award-winning photographer is brother to the McNulty sisters." Oh look here's a photo of my Mum. Now you can probably get a better idea of what she looked like with her flesh rotting off her face. Oh and look at this, "Where is the surviving sister? Our reporter goes in search of Elizabeth McNulty."

AMMY: I'm sorry.

STEWART: Just get out of my life both of you.

LUIS: Once he fuck a girl he always leave her.

STEWART: You little sod!

(*He tries to hit LUIS, AMMY tries to restrain him. There is an ugly struggle on the bed. AMMY manages to stop STEWART. Pause.*)

AMMY: Why did you bring Luis here if you're going to threaten to send him back to Brazil every time he does something wrong?

(*No response.*)

What did you expect? Huh? An instant son? Pretty naive, weren't you? It's a bit harder than that to be a parent.

STEWART: You should know. Seeing as how you don't have the time to mother your own fucking kid.

(*He goes.*)

AMMY: I'm sorry, Luis.

(*She goes to hold him. Suddenly he breaks away.*)

LUIS: This is your fault. I hate you.

(*He runs away.*

AMMY sits on the bed deflated.)

Scene 33

GIOVANNI's restaurant. STEWART and GIOVANNI. STEWART has been drinking. NOW.

GIOVANNI: That's Donna just before she went off on her travels.

STEWART: Ahha. Who's that with her? Is that…?

GIOVANNI: Liz, yes. She'd just been moved to the new place down in the Borders.

STEWART: Not Melrose?

GIOVANNI: No, it's a nursing home.

(*STEWART pours himself some more wine.*)

STEWART: You haven't changed. S'fucking amazing.

GIOVANNI: (*Referring to another photo.*) This one was taken when we went to Italy last year.

STEWART: Shit!

GIOVANNI: What?

STEWART: She's just like Kate.

GIOVANNI: Spitting image. I had a card from her yesterday. From Kathmandu. You ever been there?

STEWART: Nepal? No.

GIOVANNI: Is that where it is?

STEWART: Ay.

GIOVANNI: She says she's going to trek up some mountain.

STEWART: That's what people do in Nepal.

GIOVANNI: Ay, well, I wouldna know.

STEWART: No?

GIOVANNI: When I get away I have to go t'Italy. It's expected. You know?

STEWART: You never got to Manhattan then?

GIOVANNI: Manhattan?

STEWART: You used to talk about going there.

GIOVANNI: Did I?

STEWART: Yes. You had family there, didn't you?

GIOVANNI: Ay, I've got cousins.

STEWART: You never felt like a trip to the Big Apple?

GIOVANNI: I had my responsibilities here.

(*STEWART pours himself some more wine.*)

You like your drink then?

STEWART: Ay.

GIOVANNI: I suppose with the life you lead…

STEWART: What?

GIOVANNI: All that jetsetting. All those hotel bars, waiting for the action to start.

STEWART: Oh yeah it's just like the movies. (*Throwing out his arm.*) Very glamourous.

(*He spills wine.*

GIOVANNI gets a cloth and mops up.)

You could have come wi' me.

(*GIOVANNI says nothing.*)

I was fucking selfish. Okay? I admit it.

GIOVANNI: I wasn't saying.

STEWART: No, but you were thinking.

GIOVANNI: Mindreader as well, are you?

STEWART: Don't blame me! You chose to stay here.

GIOVANNI: Like I said, I had responsibilities.

STEWART: Yeah, well, we can't all be saints.

GIOVANNI: I'm not a saint.

STEWART: Need a pish.

GIOVANNI: That way.

> (*STEWART goes. KATE enters in prison uniform. Stirling Prison. THEN.*
>
> *GIOVANNI goes and sits opposite her.*)

I went to see the baby. At the foster home.

> (*KATE looks at him.*)

She's doing well. She can lift herself up and look at you.

> (*KATE doesn't respond.*)

I was in the restaurant yesterday. My Dad sent me there to clean up, hoover the carpet. Member the carpet? It's red and it's got they gold bits in a diamond shape? Member? So I was hoovering and I got to our spot – at the back by table number five. You'd have laughed to see me, I switched off the hoover and lay down there, just ta remember what it felt like. I closed m'eyes and imagined you were lying beside me. For a moment there I felt you beside me. I swear I could smell you there.

> (*He looks at her.*)

So, it's kept our memory, that spot.

> (*She still doesn't respond.*)

Kate?

KATE: What?

GIOVANNI: I want to look after the baby while you're in here.

KATE: Why?

GIOVANNI: Because I do. She can live wi me until you get out and then m'dad will find us a place.

KATE: She's not even yours.

GIOVANNI: I want to look after you both.

KATE: I'd make your life hell.

GIOVANNI: Course you wouldna.

KATE: It would never work.

GIOVANNI: Kate, I love you.

KATE: It's too late for that.

GIOVANNI: What d'y'mean?

KATE: I've gone cold.

GIOVANNI: Ay, well, I'll warm you then.

KATE: It will always be here now, this. Like a stone. Here.
(*She punches herself in the chest.*)
You might think that it wouldna matter. But we'd both know it was there, wouldn't we? And one night, I'd wake up and catch you looking at me like I'm a murderer.

GIOVANNI: You feel that now but in time –

KATE: (*Getting up.*) You're a fool, Giovanni. How could I live with someone as stupid as you?
(*GIOVANNI looks at her thunderstruck.*)
Don't bother coming again.
(*She goes.*
GIOVANNI goes to a point on the floor and strokes it.
STEWART returns.
GIOVANNI continues wiping up the wine.)

STEWART: You never regretted it? Taking on Donna?

GIOVANNI: No.

STEWART: Did you ever think of…

GIOVANNI: What?

STEWART: Getting a test done. To see who her father is.

GIOVANNI: I'm her father.

STEWART: I've got this son.

GIOVANNI: You said.

STEWART: I thought I could bring him over here. Be a father to him. Ridiculous.

GIOVANNI: What you going to do?

STEWART: Sending him back.

GIOVANNI: Yes?

STEWART: Unfeeling bastards don't make good parents.

GIOVANNI: Remember the day we went to the pictures the three of us?

STEWART: *Star Wars.*

GIOVANNI: Ay. And afterwards we all squeezed into one of they photo booths at the station.

(*He takes a picture from his wallet. Hands it to STEWART.
STEWART looks at it.*)

STEWART: You kept this in your wallet all these years?

GIOVANNI: Ay, it's a good photo.

STEWART: A good photo?

(*STEWART starts to weep.
KATE enters. THEN.*)

KATE: It's different for boys, isn't it? You took your chance and you got out. That's what boys do. Alright mebbe if you'd been there you could have done something. Mummy always listened to you, didn't she? Funny, isn't it? You were the only one she cared about and you were the only one who really hurt her. She got much worse after you left. And of course she took it out on us.

STEWART: If I'd known...

KATE: If you'd known? What?

STEWART: If you'd written and told me...

KATE: You'd have come back?

STEWART: Of course.

KATE: You'd never have come back. You wanted out.

(*He faces her.*)

Just make sure you look after Liz.

(*She goes.
STEWART sits shellshocked.
KATE gets in the bath.
AMMY stands singing a Trinidadian lullaby down the phone to her daughter.
KATE slits her wrists and sinks into the bath.
The lullaby continues.
After a while LIZ enters with the blackbird.
STEWART goes to her.*)

Scene 34

The nursing home garden. STEWART is watching LIZ tend the blackbird. NOW.

STEWART: What have you got there?

LIZ: My blackbird. The cat caught him and damaged his wing.

(*Pause.*)

STEWART: I'm glad you stayed in contact with Giovanni.

LIZ: And Donna.

STEWART: Yes. He said you might go and live with them.

LIZ: I can't go back there.

STEWART: Why not?

LIZ: All those articles they wrote about me.

STEWART: I'm sorry.

LIZ: People will stare at me. In the shops. In the street. They'll be worrying that I'm going to poison someone.

STEWART: You can't hide yourself away forever.

LIZ: There was a reporter came down here. He wanted to interview me. Caroline sent him packing.

STEWART: In a few weeks they'll have forgotten about it again.

LIZ: I like it here. It's safe.

STEWART: You could come and live with me, in London.

(*She looks at him.*)

LIZ: I don't know you.

(*Pause.*)

STEWART: They were supposed to look after us, Liz. They didn't look after us. You were just a child.

(*LUIS runs on with a tray of tea things. He stops when he sees them.*)

STEWART: Careful. You're spilling it.

(*LUIS puts the tea things down and goes to the bird.*
GIOVANNI enters. He has plates of ice-cream.)

GIOVANNI: I managed to persuade that tea lady to let us bring it out here. I brought us some ice-cream from the restaurant.

STEWART: Great. (*To LIZ.*) You used to love ice-cream.

(*GIOVANNI starts to pour out the tea. STEWART and LIZ watch him.*
Sound of wings fluttering. LUIS has let the bird go. They all look up.
LIZ screams.)

LIZ: He's let him go!

STEWART: You stupid –

LIZ: He's let him go. I've looked after him all this time.

LUIS: I didn't know it could fly.

STEWART: It's a bird for God's sake!

GIOVANNI: Stewart!

LIZ: The cat will get it.

GIOVANNI: He's fine.

LIZ: You don't know that.

GIOVANNI: Look. There he is, up in the tree.

STEWART: We should go.

GIOVANNI: You haven't had your tea.

STEWART: It's a long drive to London.

GIOVANNI: You can come back to Edinburgh and stay over.

STEWART: We've done enough damage.

(*LUIS starts to cry. The others all look at him.*)

GIOVANNI: Would you like to come and stay with me, Luis?

LUIS: *Eu sou um cara ruim. Tudo que eu faço é ruim.*

STEWART: You're not a bad person.

GIOVANNI: You and your Dad and your Aunty Liz can all come. Donna's coming back at the weekend. She'd like to meet you.

(*He looks at LIZ. She looks at STEWART.*)

STEWART: I don't know.

LIZ: Don't you want to meet her?

STEWART: Of course.

GIOVANNI: She's your cousin, Luis. You'll like her.

LUIS: *E melhor eu voltar pro Brasil.*

STEWART: I don't want you to go back to Brazil.

GIOVANNI: That's settled then.

(*STEWART puts his arm around LUIS. This time he is not rejected.*)

Come on. Drink your tea. And then we'll go and talk to Caroline about packing some things.

LIZ: Just for the weekend?

GIOVANNI: If you like. Oh no, look! We haven't eaten the ice-cream. It's melting. Come on.

STEWART: (*Tasting the ice-cream.*) Mmm. I like it when it's runny. Mmmm.

LIZ: Mmmm.

(*It is reminiscent of the moment with the chocolate in the bedroom.*)

LIZ/STEWART: Mmmmm.

(*They laugh.*)

ALL: Mmmm.

(*They laugh again.*
A blackbird sings. They all look up as the lights fade.)

The End.